THE INHERITORS

THE INHERITORS

Moving Forward from Generational Trauma

Belastete Kinder/Burdened Children, Paul Klee, 1930

GITA ARIAN BAACK, Ph.D.

SHE WRITES PRESS

Published 2017
Printed in the United States of America
PRINT ISBN: 978-1-63152-222-2
E-ISBN: 978-1-63152-223-9
Library of Congress Control Number: 2017934118
—Trans-Generational Trauma—Genocide —Holocaust—Memory—Resilience—Personal Narrative—Psychology—Self Help

For information, address:
She Writes Press
1563 Solano Ave #546
Berkeley, CA 94707

Cover and interior design by Tabitha Lahr

She Writes Press is a division of SparkPoint Studio, LLC.

Disclaimer: This book is set against a backdrop of complex world histories that have been written about in countless books. This book is not intended to build on, or re-create that wealth of knowledge. The utmost effort and attention has been given to ensure respectful treatment for the gravity of this subject matter.

This book is not intended to replace any therapy that a person may require.

DEDICATION

This book is dedicated to the memory of my half-brother Henush, my half-sister Helena, and their mother Hela, my father's first wife. They were murdered under the Nazi regime. There is no information or documentation about them.

Henush Arian, four years old when he was murdered

Helena Arian, three years old when she was murdered

Hela Arian, with her beloved children

This book is in honor of my indomitable mother, Lea (Laika) Alperowicz-Arian and my devoted father, Sam (Zygmunt, Zalman) Arian. They learned to speak six languages, played cards with zest and taught me to laugh and cry for no reason.

My brother, Morris, and me, my father and mother in Israel

This book salutes my *Inheritor* cohort of children who were born to parents who survived the Holocaust. I would like to say this to our generation. We are now adults and living all over the world; we may not know each other but we are intimately connected. We were given life and an obligation to bear witness. We were given a task to remind the world of the Holocaust in order to prevent hatred anywhere in the world. That is not to say that we don't have the right to live our own lives, free from the horrors of our past.

A salute also goes to *Inheritors of trauma* from around the globe who have inherited a burdensome legacy and have accepted to undertake the difficult soul work required to explore their story.

*I am interested in researching the
unfinished business in my soul and the unsaid
weight of history that waits to be said.*

—Robert Romanyshyn,
The Wounded Researcher

CONTENTS

FOREWORD

*T*he *Inheritors: Moving Forward from Generational Trauma* is a
seminal work by Dr. Gita Arian Baack, and should be read by
everyone who has encountered some form of trauma in his or her life
or who has inherited trauma. Dr. Baack's provocative book suggests
that we inherit traumas from our families and even from previous
generations, and further, that these inherited traumas influence and
impact our present life as well as future generations. She counsels that
only after we have understood these traumas can we access our feelings
of loss, grief and outrage and go on to live our lives fully.

Dr. Baack leads us on a journey over several continents and into
unknown recesses of our minds as she urges us to seek out the answers
to our inherited traumas that have impacted us to greater degrees than
we realize. She shows us the possibility of great strength and resilience
in our stories along with sadness and pain through her personal anec-
dotes, poetry and excerpts of dialogues with the *Inheritor* generations
after the Holocaust.

As an advocate for positive change, particularly regarding racism
in our communities, I found the constant theme that flows from the first
to the last page regarding the importance of dialogue between groups
and within groups, provided me with new insights on how sharing our

stories can help build understanding and solutions for current and future generations. In America, we are faced with many provocative issues that have caused immense divisiveness between "black" people and "white" people. The US election of 2016 demonstrates that racism is very much alive. However, we have not found an effective way to deal with racism because the full impacts have not been surfaced or adequately discussed, a common theme in *The Inheritors*. In the same vein we haven't explored our inherited history fully, for example, what were the impacts resulting from the disconnection from the African culture and communal way of life? What were the impacts on our social and institutional systems and on individuals resulting from 300 years of slavery?

Dr. Baack brings us an important message as she urges us to know and embrace our past in all its fullness for therein lies our hope for the future. With this understanding, *Inheritors* everywhere must engage in conversations that will help us collectively work with others to provide future generations with a better world for all of humanity.

—Herbert Merrill II, Doctorate of Education (D.Ed.); CEO, Merrill Consulting Associates, LLC; Board of Directors, Mental Health Colorado; American Counselling Association, American Psychological Association.

1

AN INVITATION TO MY READER

We are each of us angels with only one wing.
And we can only fly embracing each other.

—Luciano De Crescenzo,
Italian writer, film director, and actor

Inheritors of trauma can be defined as the generations of people who, consciously or unconsciously, have thoughts and feelings about devastating events that happened when they were very young or before they were born, or that may even go back to earlier generations.

While each of us, as an Inheritor, has followed our own unique path and has inherited our own unique stories, *Inheritors of trauma* share many similarities. How do I know? As often happens when one goes on a journey of self-discovery, I have met people from various cultures and countries whose description of their journey is similar to mine. I realized we have a universal story of *inherited trauma*, as I call it, and I call our cohort *Inheritors* or *Inheritors of trauma*. Ours is a kind of second-hand story, and it pervades our lives like deadly second-hand smoke. And like second-hand smoke, it has been invisible, often unacknowledged, but it has grievously betrayed our ability to be whole.

In speaking with other Inheritors, I often heard these key phrases: "My mother talked; my father didn't: or "My father talked, my mother didn't." "They didn't talk." or "They talked all the time." Repeated time and again by people all over the world, these phrases struck me as being more than coincidental. Generations of Inheritors of trauma everywhere are living with incomplete stories, not fully understanding why they have this sense of absence and loss.

I brought together Inheritors to talk in small groups, and I discovered that most of them have never had a chance to tell their story, not even to themselves; yet, they can easily tell their parents' stories, however complete or incomplete. As you read *The Inheritors*, we will explore many reasons that explain this. For now, let me just say that the tragic story that we have inherited usually overtakes our own story. For me, and perhaps for you, it is time to explore our own story.

The list of those who are Inheritors of trauma is long, and what follows is not necessarily a complete list. You may find yourself in more than one description:

- Inheritors are descendants of a community that has suffered from victimization and marginalization based on race, ethnicity, gender, sexual orientation, religious prejudices, dogma, and practices or government policies.
- Inheritors are the descendants affected directly or indirectly by war, armed conflict, and terrorist attacks. Given that, in the twentieth century alone, at least 108 million people were killed in wars, there are potentially countless Inheritors.
- Inheritors include descendants of the European Jewish Holocaust and Genocide and other genocides including those in Armenia, Rwanda and Burundi, Cambodia, Nanking, Croatia, Africa, India, Pakistan, Vietnam, Korea, and sadly we now include, South Sudan and Syria.
- Inheritors include the Indigenous people of Canada, the US, Australia, New Zealand, Brazil, Peru, Africa and elsewhere, who inherited a mostly unacknowledged legacy of genocide, a history of racism, degradation, and near eradication of their cultures.
- Inheritors are the descendants of African and East Indian slave traders (Portuguese, Dutch, Danish, French, and British).
- Inheritors include the loved ones of returning soldiers who came back damaged, suffering from PTSD, medicating themselves with alcohol and drugs and often committing suicide, leaving their families haunted and feeling guilty over the pain they could do nothing to heal.
- Inheritors may be the children and grandchildren of war veterans, of detention camp internees, or of prisoners in POW camps. These Inheritors proudly carry their heroic

legacy and suffering even if they do not know the details of the acts of their predecessors' heroism or martyrdom.

- Inheritors include today's 30 million children of more than 63 million fleeing refugees who helplessly struggle through harrowing experiences.
- Inheritors may be descendants of family members who were either the *perpetrators* or the *collaborators* of violence and killings. They may be carrying the guilt of this legacy, or they may have transformed the guilt into hatred and violence.
- Inheritors may be the descendants of the *bystanders*—the neighbors who saw what was happening but either didn't want to help or felt powerless to help.
- Inheritors include economic migrants, a term used by the United Nations to describe migrants who leave their country due to bad economic conditions rather than fear of persecution on the basis of race, religion, or ethnicity.
- Inheritors may come from families who have suffered the effects of natural disasters such as tsunamis, earthquakes, hurricanes, mining disasters, etc.
- Inheritors may have suffered the effects on the family of crime, sexual abuse, mental or physical illness, economic hardship, death, accidents, etc.
- Inheritors may have suffered from family difficulties, physical or mental health issues, suicide, unfair and heavy-handed treatment by government bureaucracies, courts, and institutions—i.e., the education system, health care system, internal revenue system, and large corporations.

And the list goes on . . .

People have asked me if I undertook this writing as a way of healing. My response is a clear "no!" This book is not about healing. Healing implies that there is something that is broken in us, something that needs to be fixed. We are not broken. The pathological paradigm so prevalent today leads us to think that we need to be fixed. Anti-depressants, diets, the latest gadgets, self-help books, webinars, new jargon, new gurus, new experts abound. They only give us the sense that we need help, that we are not capable, that we don't have power or a voice, and that we need all of these things to become whole. I would rather believe that, by exploring our unfinished stories, we would discover our unique resilience and our capacity for moving forward.

My invitation to you, then, is to join me in recognizing that, while we have inherited much loss, we have also inherited a capacity to move in the world with compassion and strength. Let us think of our journey together as a way of exploring our stories to help us find our common experience. My hope is that you will feel that you are neither alone nor "crazy."

During our journey together, you will listen in on some of the dialogues I held with Inheritors, giving you a glimpse of the richness of group dialogues and of the support that people give each other, often leading to new understandings and even personal transformation.

You will find that each chapter ends with questions to help you in your reflections and to discover what the stories, dialogues, and concepts presented can mean for you. I would encourage you to use these questions as you inquire about your inherited story and explore the stories of your family and members of your community. This process will help you to build a more complete picture, perhaps close some gaps in your story, and help you reframe (see a new perspective) of your understandings, emotions, and needs. You may have multiple stories with multiple reflections, and so you may want to answer the questions from various perspectives, since life is filled with rich nuances and interesting contradictions. Moving through the different aspects of our selves enables us to find the connections and the balance between past and present. I'm sure you will agree with me that the approach I offer is a far better way of talking about trauma and trans-generational trauma, a non-pathological way that opens new possibilities and new understandings.

Throughout the book, I will speak from my own personal context as an Inheritor whose parents survived the Holocaust, the most well-known genocide in history. That the killings were legally sanctioned and that industrial methods were used for mass killings make the Jewish Holocaust unique in history.

Of course there have been, and continue to be, other genocides as there have been throughout history, though the Jewish genocide was unique in a number of aspects. In Chapter Two, we will look briefly at a few of these genocides to acknowledge their existence and indicate the extent and breadth of suffering that we have, in essence, collectively inherited. While many of the illustrations of the concepts I present come from the Jewish Holocaust, I believe that what we understand about the trauma as well as the resilience experienced by Jewish Inheritors extends to the Inheritors of other holocausts and genocides.

This is a good time to move into the first set of questions that will help you write your story as we move along. Wherever you start is the right place. Whichever part of the story you want to tell is the right part. You can edit and move things around later. The ease of editing and deleting on a computer can lead you to doubt yourself, so I would recommend that you type without editing, or, better yet, do not use a computer at all. Find a notebook and write, write, write. Writing will enable you to let your thoughts and memories flow so that you won't have time to second-guess yourself. Make sure you continue writing by giving yourself permission to take even twenty minutes a day to do this important work for yourself and for the people you care about.

Trust yourself, trust your story—it will grow as it should!

Constructing Your Story

Chapter 1 Questions:
An Invitation to My Reader

- How do you feel as you set out on this journey of exploring your story?

- Who were the primary victims of your story, the survivor(s) (i.e., the First Generation) who experienced the traumatic event(s) directly?

- Where are you in the continuum? Survivor/First Generation; Second Generation (child, brother, sister, friend who inherited the trauma second-hand); Third Generation (grandchild or equivalent); Fourth Generation (great-grandchild or equivalent); Fifth Generation; Sixth Generation; more than Sixth Generation?

- What do you hope to learn or to change by reading this book?

- What do you want to stop doing, to continue doing, and to start doing with regards to your story and how it affects you?

2

GENOCIDES AND HOLOCAUSTS:
YESTERDAY AND TODAY

*So let us be alert in a twofold sense: since
Auschwitz, we know what man is capable of;
and since Hiroshima we know what is at stake.*

—Victor Frankl,
Austrian neurologist and psychiatrist, Holocaust
survivor, and author of *Man's Search for Meaning*

For centuries there have been countless massacres of designated ethnic groups, but these were not acknowledged as crimes against humanity until Rafael Lemkin, a Jew, coined the term *genocide* in 1944, in light of the Jewish Holocaust. The derivation of genocide comes from "geno," the Greek term for race, and "cide," Latin for killing.

In 1933, before the Holocaust, Lemkin made a presentation to the Legal Council of the League of Nations conference on international criminal law in Madrid, for which he prepared an essay on the "Crime of Barbarity," describing such barbarity as a crime against international law. Lemkin conceived of genocide as a *deliberate* act of persecution and destruction, not as an aberration. His definition included attacks on political and social institutions, culture, language, national feelings, religion, and the economic existence of a group. In his view, even non-lethal acts that undermine the liberty, dignity, and personal security of members of a group constitute genocide if they contribute to the weakening of the group. After the war, France added that the destruction of a culture, even though its bearers survive, also qualifies as genocide. The following information which can be found on the Genocide Watch website, outlines what is considered genocide and what are the acts that are punishable accordingly.[1]

In 1948, after the crimes against the Jewish people of Europe, the crime of genocide was defined in international law under the *Convention on the Prevention and Punishment of Genocide.* In Article II, the United Nations defined genocide as any of the following acts committed with intent to destroy, in whole or in part, a national, ethnic, racial or religious group including:

(a) Killing members of the group;
(b) Causing serious bodily or mental harm to members of
     the group;
(c) Deliberately inflicting on the group conditions of life
     calculated to bring about its physical destruction in
     whole or in part;
(d) Imposing measures intended to prevent births within
     the group;
(e) Forcibly transferring children of the group to another
     group.

In Article III, the United Nations outlined that the following acts shall be punishable:

(a) Genocide;
(b) Conspiracy to commit genocide;
(c) Direct and public incitement to commit genocide;
(d) Attempt to commit genocide;
(e) Complicity in genocide.

The Genocide Convention was adopted by the United Nations General Assembly on 9 December 1948. The Convention entered into force on 12 January 1951. More than 130 nations have ratified the Genocide Convention, and over 70 nations have made provisions for the punishment of genocide in domestic criminal law. The text of Article II of the Genocide Convention was included as a crime in Article 6 of the 1998 Rome Statute of the International Criminal Court.

The recent trials of Slobodan Milosevic in the International Criminal Court in The Hague, and of Saddam Hussein in an Iraqi court, are examples of the application of this law. In addition, an important consequence of this law is that nations have the legal right to take collective responsibility wherever there is oppression and killings of innocent people.

Today, many groups are seeking acknowledgement of the genocide against their people, including Armenians, Albanians, Indigenous people and others. As of March 2016, Genocide Watch listed on its website people at risk of genocide in the following countries: Syria, Sudan, Iraq, Somalia, Central African Republic, Rakhine and Kachin in Myanmar, Nigeria, and Burundi.

The Holocaust

One could do as one pleased only with stateless people.
—Hannah Arendt, Political Theorist, *The Origins of Totalitarianism,* and *Eichmann in Jerusalem: A Report on the Banality of Evil)*

From the 1950s onwards, the term *Holocaust* was increasingly used in English to refer to the Nazi genocide of the European Jews (or Judeocide). The terms Holocaust and Genocide became interchangeable.

The *Holocaust,* became the common term in the 1970s. Before that, this event was mostly referred to as *the war,* or in Yiddish, *de umglichkeit,* the disaster or calamity. The Hebrew word *Shoah* is preferred by many, as the origin of Holocaust from the Greek, means "burnt offering to God." Since it was not the intention of the Nazis to make a sacrifice of this kind, and since the Jews don't consider themselves to be ritual victims, the word Holocaust has been replaced with the Hebrew word *Shoah.* In North America, however, the term Holocaust is more common, so I will be using the word *Holocaust* predominantly, although *Shoah* will be used in direct quotes or dialogues.

The Holocaust describes the systematic slaughter of an estimated 6 million Jews by Nazi Germany during the specific time of World War II, 1941–1945. Along with the Jewish people of Europe, extermination and enslavement of other ethnic groups who were deemed inferior by Nazi Germany and its allies, took place during the same period, 1941–1945, bringing the total number of victims to 17.5 million. Non-Jewish Poles were the third largest group to be killed, after Polish Jews and

Hungarian Jews. The targeted people included anyone who was Jewish or had a percentage of Jewish heritage, Soviet civilians and prisoners of war, Communists, ethnic Polish, Russian, French and Dutch people, Jehovah's Witnesses, Sinti and Roma Gypsies, homosexual people, persons with physical or mental disabilities, deaf people, people with albinism, twins, political, religious, intellectual and cultural dissidents, trade unionists, and anyone who resisted Nazism.

After Germany's loss in World War I, and amid the economic wreckage, Hitler's rants found sympathetic ears and open hearts and minds that could be swayed. The Weimar Republic, a democratic government, couldn`t solve basic economic problems. President Von Hindenburg, an old and senile man, appointed Hitler to be Chancellor of Germany. It was generally believed that the Hitler regime would not last. However, with Hitler came the end of democracy. When Hitler became the all-powerful Chancellor he fooled the leaders of the democracies, who caved in to his demands. The German army occupied the Rhineland, Austria, and Czechoslovakia without real opposition from the major European powers, France and Great Britain, who scrapped their mutual defence agreement with Czechoslovakia, betraying their ally at a shameful conference in Munich in November 1938.

Then came Poland. Hitler made a non-aggression pact with Josef Stalin, and the Soviet Union and Germany became allies. The German army was free to attack Poland and within six weeks, the Polish government surrendered. For the three million Jews in Poland, it was the beginning of the end. Conditions were made unbearable under the Nuremberg laws of 1933 and Jews who had a visa from a country that would take them left in haste. Great cultural, scientific and economic leaders left. For the average citizen, it was more difficult—the free world didn't want them. The International Conference in Evian, France, in 1938 made that clear. Since no one would take in the Jews, the Nazis revised their plans when they occupied Poland, the Netherlands, Belgium, France and later the Baltic countries. In the summer of 1941, Germany invaded the Soviet Union.

Elimination gave way to extermination. The killing of the Jews in

Europe during the Second World War followed various stages for over twelve years. Coordination of the *Final Solution* policy, a policy of genocide of the Jewish people, began in January, 1942 at the Wannsee Conference, where a protocol was produced with a table of the numbers of Jews that were to be murdered in each country. Persecution of the Jews (nationals or refugees) began: economic, professional and social discrimination followed by systematic deportation and death. The complex history of the Holocaust continues to be of significance today because it offers important universal lessons for all humanity on multiple levels.

Timothy Snyder's comprehensive study in his book, *Black Earth,* reveals lessons of the Holocaust that serve as an urgent "warning call" today. The following powerful opening to Snyder's book describes why the lessons of the Holocaust are vitally important today.

"The history of the Holocaust is not over. Its precedence is eternal and its lessons have not yet been learned . . . Such a history must be colonial, since Hitler wanted wars of extermination in neighboring lands where Jews lived. It must be international, for Germans and others murdered Jews not in Germany but in other countries. It must be chronological, in that Hitler's rise to power in Germany, only one part of the story, was followed by the conquest of Austria, Czechoslovakia, and Poland, advances that reformulated the Final Solution [a plan to annihilate the Jewish race and signed into law]. It must be political in a specific sense, since the German destruction of neighboring states created zones where, especially in the Soviet Union, techniques of annihilation could be invented. It must be multi-focal, providing perspectives beyond those of the Nazis themselves, using sources from all groups, from Jews and Non-Jews, throughout the zone of killing . . . The Holocaust is not only history, but warning."[2]

Today we might see the term *holocaust* with a lower case "h" refer to mass murders and genocides, other than the Jewish Holocaust, such as the Rwandan holocaust, Cambodian holocaust, Kurdish holocaust, Bosnian holocaust, African American holocaust, and Indigenous holocaust.

In the next section, we will look specifically at two other genocides/holocausts, the Indigenous and the African American holocausts, before moving to an in-depth exploration of the impact of trauma on Inheritors. Much of what we will talk about will pertain to the various types of traumas and the various types of Inheritors listed in the opening of this book.

The Indigenous Genocide in Canada

I really don't care if you feel responsible for the past. The real question is do you feel a sense of responsibility for the future because that's what this is all about.

—Justice Murray Sinclair, Commissioner, Truth
and Reconciliation Commission

A Note about Word Usage: In Canada, the terms *Indigenous People, Aboriginal People, First Nations, or Natives,* includes the Inuit and Métis peoples of Canada under the 1982 Constitution Act. In 2007, the United Nations Declaration of the Rights of Indigenous People acknowledged the international legal rights of the Indigenous People, recognizing First Nations, Inuit and Métis as *Indigenous People.* Justice Murray Sinclair and his team used the term *Aboriginal* in the *Report of the Truth and Reconciliation Commission of Canada. First Nations* and *Native people* are also terms in use. I will respectfully use the terms Aboriginal and Indigenous interchangeably, and will also adhere to the term that is used according to the quoted reference.

The genocide of Indigenous Peoples is by far the most overlooked genocide in history. European colonization of the New World directly led to the decline of the Indigenous population by more than ninety percent, and resulted in their becoming second-class citizens in their own homeland. For hundreds of years a mixture of colonial conflict, disease, specific atrocities and policies of discrimination has devastated the native population. In the course of this time, it is estimated that over nine million Natives died from violent conflict or disease. For too long this history has been under-recognized and too little has been inadequately discussed.

In Canada, 2015 marked the tabling of the report by the Truth and Reconciliation Commission (TRC). The Commission, led by Judge Murray Sinclair, whose parents and grandparents were placed in Residential Schools, played an important role in revealing the stories that had been kept secret for so long. After six years of travelling to all parts of Canada and gathering testimony from 7,000 survivors of Christian Residential Schools and millions of documents, the Commission's legacy is now in the care of the National Centre for Truth and Reconciliation. Across the nation, 150,000 children were placed in Residential Schools, starting with the passage of the Indian Act in 1876, until 1996, when the last federally operated Residential School was closed. At least 6,000 of these students died while in attendance. This excerpt from the Truth and Reconciliation Report (now in the public domain on the internet) speaks of the legacy of the racial policies. It also speaks to the Commission's definition and use of the term *Cultural Genocide*.

"For over a century, the central goals of Canada's Aboriginal policy were to eliminate Aboriginal governments; ignore Aboriginal rights; terminate the Treaties; and, through a process of assimilation, cause Aboriginal peoples to cease to exist as distinct legal, social, cultural, religious, and racial entities in Canada. The establishment and operation of Residential Schools were a central element of this policy, which can best be described as "cultural genocide". *Cultural genocide* is the destruction of those structures and practices that allow the group to continue as a group. States that engage in *cultural genocide* set out to destroy the political and social institutions of the targeted group. Land is seized, and populations are forcibly transferred and their movement is restricted. Languages are banned. Spiritual leaders are persecuted, spiritual practices are forbidden, and objects of spiritual value are confiscated and destroyed. And, most significantly to the issue at hand, families are disrupted to prevent the transmission of cultural values and identity from one generation to the next. In its dealing with Aboriginal people, Canada did all these things . . . The negotiation of Treaties, while seemingly honourable and legal, was often marked by fraud and coercion, and Canada was, and remains, slow to implement their provisions and intent. On occasion, Canada forced First Nations to relocate their reserves from agriculturally valuable or resource-rich land onto remote and economically marginal reserves.

Canada denied the right to participate fully in Canadian political, economic, and social life to those Aboriginal people who refused to abandon their Aboriginal identity. Canada outlawed Aboriginal spiritual practices, jailed Aboriginal spiritual leaders, and confiscated sacred objects. These measures were part of a coherent policy to eliminate Aboriginal people as distinct peoples and to assimilate them into the Canadian mainstream against their will.

Aboriginal people have refused to surrender their identity. It was the former students, the Survivors of Canada's Residential Schools, who placed the Residential School issue on the public agenda. Their efforts led to the negotiation of the Indian Residential Schools Settlement Agreement that mandated the establishment of a residential school Truth and Reconciliation Commission of Canada."[3]

Disenfranchisement of Indigenous children continued into the 1950s and 60s with the forced removal of Indigenous children from their families by "Indian Agents" into foster, non-Indigenous homes, while the multi-generational trauma was still a reality. This has become known as the *Sixties Scoop*. My friend John Dione was among these children. He described the alienating effects of his separation from his families when he was placed in schools run by the Roman Catholic Church. He was not allowed to speak to his cousins, who he could sometimes see nearby, because they were considered "heathens."

The testimonies of the Residential School survivors, heard publicly and widely for the first time, were devastating. I heard one particularly cruel story about an electric chair that a priest had designed for the entertainment of visitors. Younger boys were chosen, because their little legs couldn't reach the floor, making their twitching more uncontrollable. These children were left with lifelong disabilities. In addition to physical abuse, there was also sexual and mental abuse. In most of the schools, children received little education, were beaten, starved, and forced to work. There are many undocumented deaths.

On February 14, 2017, an Ontario Superior Court judge found that Canada breached its "duty of care" when Indigenous students were forcibly taken from their homes as part of the "Sixties Scoop". The ruling paves the way for an assessment of damages (loss of identity resulting in psychiatric disorders, reduced ability to lead healthy and fulfilling lives, substance abuse, unemployment, violence and numerous suicides). The ruling will not be appealed.

At this time, there is some disagreement over the use of the term *cultural genocide* versus *genocide* when describing the Aboriginal holocaust. The Truth and Reconciliation Commission and Canadian government officials use the term *cultural genocide*. Jesse Staniforth, a Montreal-based freelance journalist and a regular contributor to the *Nation* magazine serving the Cree Nation on the eastern coast of James Bay, believes that the Aboriginal peoples experienced genocide, given the deliberate killings in the millions, forced removal of people from communities where they could hunt and fish to communities where housing was substandard and there was no source of food, intentional placement of disease-infected blankets into Indian reserves, and more such atrocities. His 2015 article published in *The Toronto Star* makes the case for using the U.N definition of genocide that we saw earlier.

> "The word cultural genocide seems to suggest that the Indian Residential Schools (IRS) system was designed to destroy cultures but not people, a fact far from the reality of Residential Schools. 'Cultural' is a civilizing adjective: it says that our policies were not truly evil, just deeply misguided . . . the IRS (Indian Residential Schools) system, though its mandate did not include deliberately killing members of Canada's Indigenous populations, was active in the following crimes, each of which constitutes genocide under the UN's convention on Genocide (1948) including: causing serious bodily or mental harm to members of the group; deliberately inflicting on the group conditions of life calculated to bring about its physical destruction in whole or in part; and forcibly transferring children of the group to another group.
>
> Canada did not pack Indigenous people onto train cars and send them to be gassed, or march them into fields and execute them with machine-gun fire. However, our country committed not "cultural" genocide, but just regular genocide. We forcibly took children from families, sometimes at gunpoint, and flew them to remote locations they could not escape, sometimes in tiny handcuffs, where they were submitted to a program of forced labour and "education" designed to destroy their cultures and civilizations . . . It is hard for Canada to admit, and announce that we are a country that committed a program of genocide that lasted for many decades."[4]

The Native American Genocide in the United States

David E. Stannard's scholarly book about Native American genocide in the U.S. and in the Americas, *American Holocaust: The Conquest of the New World,* is the product of his extensive readings, years of pondering, and fury over what Europe has wrought in America. He convincingly claims that what happened was the worst demographic disaster in the history of our species, that Old World diseases and Old World brutality drastically reduced the number of "Indians," and drove many Native American peoples over the brink of extinction. Stannard begins with a portrait of the enormous richness and diversity of life in the Americas prior to Columbus's fateful voyage in 1492. He then follows the path of genocide from the Indies to Mexico and Central and South America, then north to Florida, Virginia, and New England, and finally out across the Great Plains and southwest to California and the North Pacific Coast. Stannard underscores that wherever Europeans or white Americans went, the native people were caught between imported plagues and barbarous atrocities, typically resulting in the annihilation of ninety-five percent of their populations. The fact that disease brought by European invaders was the major cause of these deaths has been used to avoid responsibility for the extermination of so many people. He asks: "Was the exposure of Native peoples to these diseases inadvert, or was this a deliberate act?" Stannard believes that for recovery to take place we need to find out "what was crushed and what was butchered" and that missing information must be filled in before recovery can take place.[5]

In an in-depth article in the *New Republican,* titled "The Science of Suffering," about inherited trauma in various communities in the U.S., Judith Shulevitz writes: "People who have been subject to repeated, centuries-long violence, such as African Americans and Native Americans, may by now have disadvantage baked into their very molecules."[6] The same article cites the work of the anthropologist Gordon Macgregor on the predominant traits of Indigenous survivors. The traits of Indigenous survivors and their Inheritors include:

numbness, sadness, inhibition, anxiety, hyper-vigilance (over-reaction to noise, perceived potential danger), and a not-unreasonable sense that the outside world is hostile.

We will be gathering descriptions of traits of Inheritors for three groups: Holocaust survivors, African Americans, and Indigenous people. Maria Yellow Horse Brave Heart, a student of the Indigenous genocide in the US and a Lakota professor of social work, called these traits *unmourned loss*.[7] (The subject of grief and mourning will be explored in Chapter Six.)

In more recent times, American Native people in the U.S., like their Indigenous counterparts in Canada, were disenfranchised and traumatized by being removed from their families and placed in boarding schools under racist policies. These children died of tuberculosis, were humiliated, beaten, and raped. They were not allowed to speak their language or to practice their traditions. Their names were changed, and in so doing, they lost their most fundamental source of identity. In the U.S. and in Canada and many other aboriginal peoples throughout the world, suffer from poverty, poor health, homicide, high rates of suicide, and other serious issues.

America's Black Holocaust Museum (ABHM)

Dr. James Cameron founded America's Black Holocaust Museum (ABHM) after visiting *Yad Vashem*, the Holocaust Memorial Museum in Jerusalem, Israel. He noted many similarities between the experiences of the Jewish people and African Americans and identified the cruel elements that we share, such as:

- Forced marches and migrations;
- Stolen property;
- Dehumanization;
- Slave labor;
- Mass incarceration;

- Torture;
- Medical experimentation;
- Discrimination;
- Race riots (similar to the *pogroms* in Europe);
- Lynchings;
- Mass murder;
- Long-lasting psychological effects (Post-Traumatic Stress Disorder) on survivors and descendants.

Dr. Cameron admired how Jewish people value their history and educate themselves and others about it, and he saw how this gave the Jewish people strength. He wanted the same for African Americans and created the *America's Black Holocaust Museum* to contain a comprehensive history and exploration of the past four-hundred-year history of the Black holocaust and to serve as a memorial for the descendants.

The African American history, summarized below, is excerpted from the site of *America's Black Holocaust Museum.*[8]

The Black holocaust in America began in the 1600s with the first settlements in Virginia, where laws were passed making black people, and only black people, slaves for life. Ten to twelve million African men, women, and children were kidnapped from their homes and forced to march as many as one thousand miles to the sea. There they were held in underground dungeons for up to a year. The kidnapped people were packed below decks as cargo on 54,000 slave ship voyages to the Americas. They were usually shackled and unable to move. These trips, called "The Middle Passage," constituted one of the largest forced migrations in world history. When the captives arrived in America, men, women, and children—even infants—were put on the auction block at slave markets. The buyers handled them as if they were cattle. Children were often sold away from their parents, and husbands from their wives.

By the time of the US Civil War in 1861, eight generations of black children had been born, had grown up, toiled, and died as the property of white adults and their children. Slaves worked at hard labor for no pay. They were frequently whipped, and were not allowed to learn reading, writing, or arithmetic. They were poorly fed, housed, and clothed. Many of their daughters, sisters, and wives were raped. Many saw their children, spouses, parents, siblings, and friends sold away. And there was no hope of an end to their suffering.

The Thirteenth Amendment to the US Constitution outlawed slavery, but many of the four million former slaves were forced back into unpaid labor. They became sharecroppers on their old plantations. If a white man said a black man was shiftless, that black man could be arrested and forced to work without pay in a mine, factory, or farm. This was slavery by another name.

After emancipation came the separate and unequal system of Jim Crow in the South. This made it legal to racially segregate public schools, buses, restaurants, movie theaters, and occupations. Under Jim Crow, black lives were cheap. Over five thousand African Americans were strung up, shot, tortured, mutilated, and burned to death during those one hundred years.

The Civil Rights Movement of the 1950s, 60s, and 70s challenged Jim Crow. The Jim Crow era officially ended when Congress passed the Civil Rights Act of 1964; however, white Americans found ways around many of the gains African Americans made. White parents moved to the suburbs or put their children in private schools. White neighbors signed covenants not to sell their homes to black families. White unions made it difficult for black workers to become members and to advance themselves in the skilled trades. Many African Americans became trapped in poverty.

The history and breadth of the African *diaspora* (exile, expulsion, dispersal or displacement of a people from their original homeland) is not well known. Between 1500 and 1900, approximately four million enslaved Africans were transported to island plantations in the Indian Ocean, about eight million were shipped to Mediterranean-area countries, and about eleven million survived the Middle Passage to the New World. Countless others did not survive. Their descendants are now found around the globe, but for various reasons such as intermarriage, they are not necessarily readily identifiable.

Another museum, *From Enslavement to Mass Incarceration,* expected to open in 2017, will be the first museum in the US dedicated to defining, understanding, and accepting slavery and the widespread lynching of African Americans. It is the initiative of a prisoners' rights group, *The Equal Justice Initiative (EJI)* under the leadership of Bryan Stevenson. He discusses the need for the US to confront some of the darker realities of its past: "I think it's important because when you do that, you change your identity, you change your relationship to these histories of mass atrocities and violence. But when you don't do that, things linger. The smog created by that history of racial inequality continues to compromise our health. And in this country, we haven't done that about slavery, about lynching or about segregation."[9] Looking at current shocking incarceration data in the U.S. including: the highest rate of incarceration in the world, 6 million people on probation or parole, 1 in 3 black male babies born in this country is expected to go to jail or prison, Stevenson concludes that there is a line from slavery to racial terrorism through segregation that is evident in what we see in our criminal justice system.[10]

Beverly Greene, one of the editors of the anthology *Psychotherapy with African American Women,* describes the holocaust that was the African American experience: "My parents are survivors of an American holocaust, the Mississippi and Georgia of the 1920s through the late 1940s. For those unfamiliar with the racism of the rural south, my father's walk to school would include passing a tree whose branches had strange fruit. *Strange fruit* was a term made famous by the Billie Holiday classic of the same name, calling up the macabre images of the Southern lynch mobs. Strange fruits were the dead bodies of Black men hanging by the neck, often castrated and visibly disfigured."[11]

In *"The Courage to Heal: African American Women's Memories of Racial Trauma,"* an important chapter in the Jackson and Greene anthology discussed above, Jessica Henderson Daniel focuses on understanding racism as a reality-based and repetitive trauma in the lives of African American women. The title, *"The Courage to Heal,"* calls on therapists to be open to, and to listen to, experiences of racism.

She believes that most European white therapists fail to do so, partly because of a lack of training about racism in educational institutions that are racially biased, and partly because of their own discomfort with the subject. Daniel views the reluctance to speak about racism and racist memories by White Americans, which she calls *racial silence,* is because to do otherwise would be to break open the myth of meritocracy—that is, should White Americans admit that they benefit from the privilege of their white skin at the expense of others, it would be a threat to their self-worth. Some excuses used at the personal level are that they don't know how to speak up or that things are so much better, e.g. "we don't use the 'N-word' anymore."[12]

Jessica Henderson Daniel also provides an in depth discussion of a number of different types of historical racial traumas that reverberate intensely when they recur or appear in the media today. For example, the Clarence Thomas–Anita Hill Senate Hearings in the US highlighted racial silencing of sexual victimization "for the good of the race" and black women's vulnerability to racial abuse. "The traumatic memories stimulated by the hearing were two-fold: the initial victimization and then the denial of it . . . The constructions and reconstructions of the African American woman have effectively limited society's perceptions of women as victims but has also limited Black women's perception of the legitimacy of their victimizing experiences. Denial of the victim state compounds the trauma."[13]

Daniel discusses the different areas impacted by historical racial trauma, including: sexual trauma (regular experiences of sexual harassment); racial violence (church burnings, KKK); trauma experienced in the judicial and law enforcement systems (police brutality, false accusations, wrongful or extreme sentencing of black men); trauma experienced in the educational system (poor quality of education, assumption of intellectual inferiority); trauma experienced by the medical system (denial of treatment); and racial trauma caused by the economic system (in employment and housing).

Again, the descriptions of the survivors' reactions to these traumas are similar to those of survivors of the Holocaust. In some cases, they do not speak about their family's history of violence or murder in order to protect their offspring from painful stories. In other cases, these stories are told to warn of the potential danger in encountering angry whites and to teach docility when speaking with police. The Inheritor generation grows up with a sense of danger and an understanding that they cannot depend on the protection of white society.

Daniel stresses that the negative impacts of racial trauma are serious and trans-generational, and must be addressed at all levels.[14] This list of the resultant traits of racial trauma are synthesized from Daniel's discussions:

- Self-hatred and low self-esteem;
- Anger/moral outrage, anxiety and avoidance;
- Distrust of white people, authorities, the justice system and law enforcement officers;
- Lack of trust and respect in inter-racial relations;
- A sense of physical and psychological vulnerability;
- A state of hyper-vigilance: Don't let your guard down;
- Low level of confidence in academic skills.

Recently there have been studies on racial policies and practices aimed at terrorizing and subjugating Black men and killing them as well. One such study discusses the recent shootings of black men by police. Samuel R. Aymer compares these killing with lynchings in his research article, "I Can't Breathe: A Case Study—Helping Black Men Cope With Race-Related Trauma Stemming From Police Killing And Brutality".[14]

It would be most interesting if African American Inheritors, Indigenous Inheritors and Holocaust Inheritors were to meet and share their stories. I am certain they would find much in common and also learn from one another. A collective *re-storying* of these histories is critically needed to deconstruct the theory in practice of power and hierarchy.

Constructing Your Story

Chapter 2 Questions:
Genocides and Holocausts: Yesterday and Today

- In your family and ancestral family, what stories have you heard?

- What are the impacts on you of their stories and traumatic experiences?

- Do any of the traits of trauma described fit for you or members of your family?

- What do you think still needs to be done at the national, state, community, and family levels?

3

KNOWING, NOT KNOWING

*Every heart, every heart
to love will come
but like a refugee.*

—Leonard Cohen,
from the song *Anthem*

As we move into an exploration of the impacts of traumatic events on subsequent generations, let me introduce you to a simple drawing that will accompany us on this journey. The Swiss artist, Paul Klee, created *Burdened Children* in 1930. The drawing shows children who survived World War I. My discovery of this drawing was a stroke of luck or serendipity, as I like to say. When I visited the Tate Modern Gallery in London, England, I had just begun to think about writing this book. As I arrived at the gallery, I had the intuition that I would find a piece of art that would help me. When I came across Klee's drawing, I was dumbstruck. This little line drawing, so simple and at the same time so complex and aptly titled, perfectly captures what it means to be a child after a traumatic event. May you, with the help of this drawing, find insights into your own unique experience. Let us begin this journey together inspired by the forward movement depicted by these children.

My Beginnings: A Displaced Persons Camp

Belonging to a race that was almost exterminated, I was born in a Displaced Persons (DP) camp. Like the children in Paul Klee's drawing, I began my life in the aftermath of a world war.

My parents met in the midst of World War II. They were an unlikely couple, the butt of a running joke amongst their friends: How could it be that a *Litvak* (someone from the city of Vilna in Lithuania) would ever marry a *Galicianer* (someone from the city of Kraków in Galicia, Poland), given the well-known differences attributed to these two communities? But like many other couples in desperate circumstances, theirs was a necessary alliance, forged in the midst of terror and fear, with the primary intention of survival. It is possible they were married in a city hall in the town of Gorczakowo in Uzbekistan. When questioned about their wedding, my parents would not answer me, only chuckling in response. Since my father didn't know at the time whether his wife, Hela, and their two young children, Henush and Helena, were alive, in normal circumstances, their union would have been considered illegal. But, apparently, such civil ceremony marriages were not uncommon.

Romance had little to do with my parents' relationship, which grew more and more contentious with the years, yet their loyalty to one another was unshakeable. After the war, my mother accompanied my father to his home in Kraków. My mother was prepared to leave if they discovered that his wife was still alive. I don't know how, probably someone told them that my father's wife and children had been killed. It may be that my mother was already pregnant with me during that trip or at least shortly after. So many gaps!

The Displaced Persons Camp (DP camp or refugee camp) where I was born was in Wasserburg, am Inn, Bavaria, Germany. Originally a monastery, it had been converted for Jewish refugees after the Holocaust. My mother would joke that I was manufactured in Poland and produced in Germany. Like me, a quarter of a million people were in DP camps between 1945 and 1947, many unable to leave for years. Jews became Displaced Persons (DPs) and spent time in helter-skelter camps, some of which were located at former concentration camps. Conditions in the camps were dismal. Many survivors had no method of contacting relatives, as they were not allowed to send or receive mail. Victims slept in their bunkers, wore their camp uniforms, and were not allowed to leave the barbed-wire camps, while the German population outside of the camps was able to return to normal life. The military reasoned that the victims (now prisoners) should not be allowed to roam the countryside for fear that they would attack civilians, though the opposite was true: civilians frequently attacked the frail survivors.

My family's situation was much better. According to my mother, we were treated very well, because I was the most beautiful baby in the camp. Physical attractiveness remained important to my mother throughout her lifetime because for her, it meant the difference between survival and death. The more likely reason for our good treatment was that this DP camp was officially managed by the UN aid organization, United Nations Relief and Rehabilitation Administration (UNRRA), and unlike most DP camps, the inhabitants were allowed considerable autonomy. This small medieval town served as a refuge for a few thousand survivors from Poland, Hungary, Romania, and Czechoslovakia. When I contacted the Archivist of Wasserburg, I learned that between 1946 and 1950, its population included up to 2,000 Jews, including 250 children and teenagers. There were schools and opportunities for the adults to learn a trade.

Though the war was over, my mother continued to encounter hardship. She described herself as entering the DP camp pregnant and frail, with only a small bundle that carried all her possessions. She had food stamps, but she was too weak to stand in line. My father had met some friends, and seemed to prefer their company to hers. She was not the same woman who, a few years earlier at age twenty-two, was full of passion and involved with many organizations and cultural events. Now that the worst was over, she had no more strength left and no one to support her; even my father seemed unavailable.

I imagine that she wondered about the unfairness of it all, and might have said to herself:

"My husband doesn't care about me. I am alone in the

world! Why did this happen to me? Hadn't I saved my husband's life by bribing a judge when he was jailed for stealing
bread and sick with malaria? Hadn't I saved my brother when
I found him in East Russia without money and with a wound
along his entire leg? Hadn't I charmed people into helping us?
What if he abandons me now? I have a baby on the way. How
will we survive? I'm so scared and alone. This isn't fair!"

(I will talk more about her story of escape in Chapter 8 on resilience.)

My father's story is more difficult to put together, because he
didn't speak about it. I sensed his suffering in the same way I sensed
my mother's suffering. Intuiting the feelings of our survivor parents,
despite their silences and all that remains unspoken, is a common ability among children of survivors. Today, I understand more fully that
my father's apparently cold reaction to my mother was probably due
to the shock of having recently learned about the death of his wife and
children. Just a few short years before he had been married to another
woman, and the father of two beautiful children. He must have had to
numb his feelings of grief and guilt.

I can only imagine how unprepared he was to be starting a new
family so soon after learning of the death of his wife and children. There
certainly was no grief counselling, no way of processing his loss and
grief. I imagine he must have been questioning his decisions and his
new wife's seemingly unreasonable demands:

"Hadn't I saved her life by stealing hot bread from the oven,
burning my legs where the bread was hidden under my
socks? Hadn't I gone to prison when I was turned in for
stealing? Hadn't I married her as we fled on false documents?
Doesn't she understand my pain for betraying my own wife
and children? I don't know if I want to go on."

(I will talk more about his story of escape in Chapter 8 on
resilience.)

Like the many baby-boom births following the war, we were all little miracles. A woman's ability to conceive after the war was a paradoxical miracle. During the war, many women experienced a cessation of menses/period. I once asked my mother what women did during the war when they had their period. I was stunned by her answer: they didn't have a monthly period. She attributed this to hunger. I now have learned that this is a documented phenomenon and more than likely relates to fear and traumatic stress.[1]

My given names, Gita Arian, are filled with ironies, a kind of prediction of the contradictions I would be sorting out throughout my life. My namesake, my father's beloved mother, Gita, was killed by the Nazis, though the details of her death remain unknown. My surname was Arian. Didn't Hitler exterminate the Jews in order to ensure a pure Aryan race? Some of our documents, including versions of my birth certificate, have a Polish/Dutch spelling of *Arjan*—not much better. When I started high school, I changed my name from Gita to Ginny, but changed it back when I went to university. I have come to like both my first name and last name. In fact, I know now that Arian is inscribed as a bona fide Jewish name in the city of Kraków, and has been for many generations. I also like the way "Gita" evokes India and the Bhagavad Gita; I believe we are all people of the world, not separated by borders, race or religion. My name has provided me with some wonderful conversations.

I feel that I came into the world as a wise, sad child. I always knew that I was a child of parents who miraculously survived a catastrophe, "survived" in a manner of speaking. I knew that their losses were immense, though barely articulated, their wounds unspeakable and unappeasable. I knew emotionally what I didn't—couldn't as a child—really understand. But still I understood. Their loss was my loss, and that loss seeped into my core.

Sandor Ferenczi, a Hungarian psychoanalyst and close friend of Freud, published a paper titled "The Dream of the Clever Baby," in which he identified a phenomenon he had discovered through his clinical work: the notion that traumatized young children often had accelerated developmental characteristics, including highly acute sensitivities and intuitions—in short, wisdom beyond their years. He characterized them as "wise" babies, saying, "We should not forget that the young child is familiar with much knowledge, as a matter of fact, that later becomes buried by the force of repression."[2] As I have worked with people to reconstruct their legacies, I have found that we are commonly faced with the conundrum of memory and knowing what cannot be known.

From my earliest beginnings, I remember carrying a great sadness for my siblings, Henush and Helena, who were only four and three years old when they were killed. I have never been able to think about them or speak their names without choking up. There are no burials, no documents, and no information about the date or circumstances of their deaths. My father told me their ages when they died, and I have approximated the year based on my research about the Kraków ghetto and the killings there. There are no bodies, no spots to mark their graves. But their existence was real and has mattered to me in an extraordinary way. And so I don't fight the sadness; I embrace it. It has a special place. I am the carrier of their memory. This burden is the most cherished of all my burdens. I see myself in Klee's drawing as a child carrying this precious burden.

The next chapter discusses some fascinating forms that memory can take. As you read these descriptions, make note of any seeds of new possibilities of the unknown that you may notice, no matter how small. I will be doing the same, curious to see where these threads of learning might help me know what happened to my brother and sister, Henush and Helena.

Constructing Your Story

Chapter 3 Questions: Knowing, Not Knowing

- In Klee's drawing, what burdens do you see the children carrying?

- How did you begin your life?

- How did you get your name? Who were you named after? What is the significance of your name and how do you feel about it?

- Where were your parents born? How did they meet?

- Did you and your parents need to move to another region or another country?

- When you were born what were your parents' emotional state (what have you been told and what do you suspect)?

- What are the things you know for sure, and what have you always sensed or thought to be true but don't really know for sure? What impact has not knowing had on you?

4

DIFFERENT FORMS OF MEMORY

Memory allows you to have continuity in your life . . . it is our most precious mental ability because if you don't have memory, you don't care about anything else.

—Eric Kandel, MD,
Nobel Laureate in Physiology/Medicine

There are forms of memory that can help us to reconstruct our story or that can give us closure about the unknowns in our story. I believe that there are also forms of memory that can help us access knowledge that we didn't realize we had. After reading these theories about the different forms memory can take, including my own theory of *inherited memory*, you can answer for yourself the question that began my search:

Do we carry memory from one generation to another?

Inherited Memory

Brothers and sisters are as close as hands and feet.
—Vietnamese Proverb

There are different ways of knowing, and there are different forms of not knowing. We don't have access to all of our psyche and emotions. And generally, we don't know what we don't know and we don't know *that* we don't know. Let us entertain the possibility that there is knowledge and information that is neither external nor scientific, but that we hold within our bodies and minds in ways that are not easily accessible. We will explore some of these possible doors to hidden knowledge through different forms of memory.

My own experience provides an example. My half-siblings, Henush and Helena, to whom I dedicate this book, were among the 1.5 million children who were murdered under the Nazi rule. (I feel as though they are fully my brother and sister, so I won't use the term "half-siblings" in the rest of the book.) I will likely never find any tangible information or gain a factual accounting of what happened to Henush and Helena. I can tell you, however, that I know exactly what happened, even though I cannot account for it through documents or witnesses.

Since I was a child, as young as five years old, I have had a *knowing*. This knowing is lodged in a spot in the middle of my back. My knowing, which I call my *inherited memory*, tells me that my brother and sister died from being shot in the back by Nazi soldiers.

When I was older, I asked my father about his children's deaths. He told me he didn't know how they were killed, so he couldn't understand why I thought they were shot. He said we can't possibly know. What I didn't tell him was that my knowing comes from a spot in the middle of my back that feels like a memory of being shot there. I wasn't more than about eight years old at that time, and the memory went back much earlier still.

I have always reacted intensely if someone touches that spot. Sometimes I had nightmares of something pressing hard on my back, and I would feel an agonizing pain that I couldn't stop. I would wake up, surprised and relieved to find that it was a dream. About ten years ago, during a visit to my acupuncturist, Dr. James Wayling, I asked him to avoid putting any needles on this special spot in the middle of my back, since I would likely faint or jump if he did. When I explained to him the reason behind my peculiar request, my acupuncturist knowingly replied, "Yes, we are more connected with our siblings than we realize." For the first time, I felt understood by someone and I started to believe that there was a possibility that my felt sense was in fact real. Not being a person with much of a spiritual bent, this was highly unusual for me. Neither am I a follower of the rational, scientific approach to the mysteries of life. The scientific methodology is too mechanical and too narrowly focused for these questions. I do believe we are all connected and that we have a wisdom that is much greater than we give ourselves credit for. I have acquired a philosophical stance based on much thought and a variety of readings. One of the most influential constructs comes from my Advisor, Kenneth Gergen, of the Taos Institute, and a world leader in the theory and practice of Social Construction. Social Construction speaks to the idea that the source of meaning, value and action is in the relational connection among people. It is through relational processes that we create the world in which we most want to live and work.[1] Everything we know comes from our interactions with others. That is one of the reasons that I believe in the potential of group dialogues for transforming emotional and mental distress, misunderstanding caused by words and conflict in relationships. (More about dialogues later.)

And so, free of pre-determined constructs in the pursuit of understanding my connection with my brother and sister, I look for more clues. One clue has been there all along. My brother, Morris and I share an uncanny coincidence in our birthdates with Henush and Helena. All four of us have birth dates that correspond. We were all born on the twenty-third day of the month. Helena was born October 23, while I was born the following month on November 23; my half-brother, Henush, was born December 23, while my brother, Morris, was also born the following month, January 23. Further research, as you will see, continued to corroborate my inherited memory.

You could say that my research into the history of my siblings began in Canada when I was still a child. I felt I was living a kind of abnormal life in the midst of normal life. Every time I saw a newsreel at the cinema or on television, I would look closely at the faces in the pictures, hoping to find a glimpse of my siblings. I was lucky—I had a picture of them and I knew what they looked like. My father and mother must have brought this photo back with having left Uzbekistan to return to my father's city of Krakow, to determine if his wife and his children might still be alive. They might have even gone into the house where my father had lived with his wife and children, and gathered those pictures, or perhaps a neighbor had kept them. This is one of many gaps in my parents' war story that I cannot fill.

I now know that one reason I haven't been able to find any information on the children is that no records regarding children who were under five years of age were kept. I also found out the chilling reason why young children were killed immediately. Along with the fact that they could not be put to work, Heinrich Himmler, chief of the S.S., declared on October 6, 1943, that it would not be wise to exterminate adult Jewish men and women, and allow their children to grow up to become avengers. For this very bizarre reason, the decision was made to annihilate every Jewish child as well as the adults. It was the first time in history that children were specifically targeted for annihilation.[2] Unfortunately, it was not the last time children were targeted, as we know from the targeting of children in the Rwandan genocide of 1994, and for a similar reason: they didn't want witnesses.

My search for any information about Henush and Helena, or about their mother, Hela, has been an increasingly hopeless quest. Letters to archives in Germany and Poland have come back with regrets that there is no information; database searches have found no trace of them (nor of other members of my father's family or my mother's family). What I have been able to piece together is that my father's wife and children were likely killed between 1941 and 1943, probably before the transports of the Kraków Jews to the death camps of Belzec and Auschwitz began. This is what I learned about what transpired during that time that leads me to think this.

During the inter-war years, having a well-established Jewish community of around 60,000, the city of Kraków was a center of Jewish cultural life. The Kraków ghetto was officially established in March 1941. Two major camps were constructed nearby: the labor camp, Plaszów, and the death camp, Auschwitz, only forty miles away.

Inside the Kraków ghetto, people were crammed together in harsh conditions, with little food. Those who were able to work were employed in factories set up in the ghetto or in surrounding areas of the city. The most famous of these was the factory of Oskar Schindler, whose efforts to save the lives of his Jewish workers were made famous in Steven Spielberg's film, *Schindler's List*.

It is likely that my siblings and their mother were taken to the Kraków ghetto around 1941. This was before the gas chambers were built. Given that children under five were killed immediately (as were the old and disabled), and since the gas chambers did not yet exist, I believe that this provides further evidence that my brother and sister were indeed shot.

Snyder's book, *Black Earth*, mentioned earlier, includes this description of the cold-blooded shooting of children. Considering I previously had no way of knowing that children were shot, this vivid and chilling revelation eerily reinforces my inherited nightmare:

> "Stahlecker, the commander of *"Einsatzgruppe A"* (death squads primarily by shooting) recognized that the murder of civilians was an 'emotional strain.' Extra alcohol was given to German men who shot Jewish children, but that was not enough . . . In the Nazi press, a key idea from Hitler's, *My Struggle,* was brought to public attention in July 1941: that the Jews must be annihilated because they wish to kill all Germans . . . The idea that it was the enemy that was guilty of policies of extermination, [meant] their deeds were nothing more than self defense. It took weeks to shift from killing a few women and older children to killing them all . . . Local Lithuanians, Poles and Russians [were recruited] to assist in the shooting . . . To shoot babies in Mahileu [part of the Soviet Union that is now in Belarus] was, as one man explained to his wife, to prevent something worse: 'During the first try I aimed calmly and shot surely as many women, children and infants. I kept in mind that I have two infants at home, whom these hordes would treat just the same, if not ten times worse. The death that we gave them was a beautiful quick death . . . Infants flew in great arcs through the air, and we shot them to pieces in flight, before their bodies fell into the pit and into the water.'"[3]

What a trial it has been to piece together my personal tragedy. I have come up against legal, bureaucratic, and technical obstacles to finding information. I am not alone. Inheritors often take on the role of researcher in their diligent attempts to recreate their lost cultures and their family histories. A fellow Inheritor, Judith Maier, whose parents gave testimonials in a variety of war crime trials, said to me, "One day I intend to find all these testimonies." One of the dialogue participants told me that, by putting the pieces together of her father's story, "I hope to honor my father by knowing what I do not know." There are countless volunteers helping to research and fill databases with information on those who have perished. Genealogy conferences are typically filled with fascinating programs and attended by large numbers of participants.

Given the magnitude of research to be done, I expect the process of recreating lost history will continue for many years—many generations, in fact. Perhaps this is an example of our resilience in the form of tenacity, pushing against walls of indifference and obfuscation. Perhaps Klee's searching children are walking through walls that have been put up before them, and perhaps we can note a slight smile of triumph as they proceed.

Memory as Family Stories

Along with inherited memory there are other forms of memory, conscious and unconscious, that serve us in recreating our histories. A common form of non-experiential memory is the kind of memory we create from stories we are told by others about ourselves. We often accept these and make them our own, or at least, believe them to be true. This kind of memory has been identified as *false memory* by neuroscientists; I don't think there is anything false about it. These stories are integral to our identity, and even if they are partly mythical, they have created a meaning that is equivalent to a memory for us.

Silent Memory

Dr. Carol Kidron, an anthropologist with Haifa University, developed one view of memory work. In Kidron's work with Holocaust descendants in Israel and with children of the Cambodian genocide survivors in Canada, she found that it is the everyday experiences of survivors and their descendants that provide us with memory. She calls this *silent memory,* and defines it as "a knowing without words, narrative or history." She also prefers to think of this as *presence* rather than as *absence,* a common description of the trans-generational experience.[4]

An obvious example of familial *silent memory* is the sense that our parents knew hunger even though they didn't tell us directly. For people outside the family (and even within the family), it is hard to understand this if they aren't attuned to possible meanings beneath the parents' behaviour. Seeking to understand how a non-Inheritor person might react to or parents, I asked one of the participants about her non-Inheritor husband. In this excerpt from one of my dialogues, we clearly see, as does the Inheritor child, that the parent has known hunger; yet, a non-Inheritor person—in this case the husband of an Inheritor—could not understand the behavior of his wife's traumatized father.

> **GITA:** Kathi, how did your husband react to your parents? Did they seem weird to him?
>
> **KATHI:** At first he looked down on them; he may have picked it up from me, but since his parents are gone there is a 100 percent change. My father, who was kind, would offer Marc food and drink, which he would refuse. My father kept offering and Marc got mad and yelled, "How many times do I have to tell you I don't want anything."

I have observed that immigrant children, like Kathi and myself, regularly take on the role of interpreting the world to their parents because of differences in language and culture, and because the parents' worldview is often based on their devastating experiences and can't be understood by those who aren't attuned to it. On the other hand, we also have to translate and interpret our parents to others, especially since they often also speak with accents that are difficult for others to understand. My ex-husband, who was not Jewish and was from Minnesota, would often inadvertently insult my parents. One day, he casually put his feet on the table as he was talking to my mother. She was highly insulted at this breach of respect and was furious. This was simply a cultural misunderstanding. On his part, he was very patient and learned to put up with my mother's constant worries and many phone calls.

Like all immigrants, we write checks for our parents, we make phone calls, we explain teacher's report card comments, and we run interference with authorities that our parents have learned to fear.

The knowledge and the behaviors resulting from silent memory can also be passed down to future generations. Using the same example of hunger, I admit that I too have acquired the habit of not wasting food. This illustration might sound a bit bizarre. I noticed that, as my son was preparing strawberries, he was throwing out strawberry bits that he chopped off at the top along with the green stem. When no one was looking, I took the strawberries out of the garbage, carefully cut out the green bits, and made myself a bowl of with the parts of the strawberries that had been thrown away. I could not stand to see those bits of strawberries sitting in the garbage.

My parents spoke of knowing hunger, but what they didn't know was how hunger was used as a tactic to control both the Soviet civilians and the Jews. Snyder explains that the possibility of starvation was an issue for Russians and Poles. "In the process of Nazi decision-making about the fate of Polish Jews, one relevant calculation became Jewish productivity versus Jewish consumption of calories. At moments when saving food seemed more pressing, Jews were killed; at moments when labor seemed more urgent, Jews were spared."[5] The promise of food was used in various ways, from enticing Jews to centers for deportation or for recruiting collaborators, even Jewish collaborators.

Phantom Memory

You can drive the devil out of the garden, but you will find him again in the garden of your son.
　　　　—Heinrich Pestalozzi, Social Reformer and Educator
　　　　known as "the father of modern education"

I find this description by Alice Miller of what happens to the child when they sublimate their needs for the sake of the needs of their parents, to be a clear description of phantom memory. Miller said: "One could say that it is the split off and un-integrated parts of the parents that have been introjected in the child."[6]

A good way to begin discussing the rather complex phenomenon of *phantom memory* is with a story about Judith Kestenberg as told by Esther Rashkin, wherein she relates that Judith Kestenberg could tell from the way a person held their body whether they were a Holocaust survivor, or from a painting, if the artist was a second generation child of survivors. Rashkin tells this story:

"We went with Judith [Kestenberg] to see a new exhibition of paintings in Jaffa. Judith stood in front of a portrait of a man for a long time, and then told me, 'You see, this is a child survivor. Look at the sad eyes, the expression on the face. . .' We asked the painter about the portrait, and he told us it was of his father, who was present at the event. Judith asked the artist's father if he was a child during the Second World War. The man, who looked and spoke like an English gentleman, was speechless. He acknowledged being a Holocaust survivor, but warned us that his son did not know about it. He asked Judith how she found out about it, and Judith said that through the portrait that was painted by his son, she was able to detect all the hidden suffering that his son knew about without knowing that he knew. Later, the father was finally able to talk to his son."[7]

We have to ask: *What did the son know that his father didn't tell him? How did he know? Why is it important that he knew?* Rashkin, whose work intersects psychoanalytic theory and practice and popular culture, literature, film, and dance, would answer these questions as follows. A type of transmitted traumatic neuroses is at work in some children of Holocaust survivors. She calls this *transposition,* wherein the survivor's child goes beyond identification with the parent and transposes himself or herself into the parents' past, playing out the various roles in that past with the unconscious intention "to change the past and convert the parents' suffering and guilt into victory over the oppressors."[8]

Rashkin proposes a *phantomogenic* (meaning unrecognizable) source of transmission of distress. After examining literary texts and film narratives, she developed a theory centered around unspeakable secrets that are so shameful, conflicted, and destabilizing to the psyche, that they need to be hidden and yet still preserved. She suggests that, to release the phantoms from their state of preservation in the recesses of the psyche, one must speak about the secret so that one is able to move forward. Once the secret is revealed and spoken, the drama will be silenced and will not be transmitted trans-generationally.[9]

Another fascinating type of phantom memory discussed by Rashkin relates to Abraham and Torok's work on the *intrapsychic crypt* (like a tomb, but in the mind). They describe a situation when language is blocked because of a loss or a shameful trauma that is too distressing to speak about. The loss or secret is sealed up alive in the *intrapyschic crypt.* The crypt serves as an isolating mechanism to keep the loss or secret from exposure. The person, therefore, cannot only avoid mourning the loss or acknowledge the shame, but can also deny that any loss has taken place.[10] The transmission by the parent, who concealed the disturbing event, can occur through language and behavior directly onto the child. The child then becomes a repository of an unspeakable trauma experienced by someone else.

The phantom can also haunt the family through successive generations, and can even skip generations and be transmitted from parent to a grandchild. The child may be diagnosed as obsessive, compulsive, phobic, hysterical, eating-disordered, manic, depressive, schizo-phrenic, autistic, etc. "The haunted child becomes the unwitting. . . agent of a gap in speech of the parent. . . that blocks the child from liv-ing life as her or his own. . . and [becoming] an independent being."[11]

It is difficult to analyze *phantomogenic transmissions*, since in fact the person has no memory or knowledge of the secreted event. But it is possible that a person's eating disorder may be a result of transferring their parent's experience of starvation, or it may be a phantomogenic transmission, for example, from their mother's unspeakable shame for prostituting herself for food.[12]

Phantom memories are transmitted in response to many differ-ent kinds of catastrophes. Along with Inheritors of the victimized, Inheritors of the persecutors are also susceptible to these kinds of transmissions. Such persecutors include Argentinian military and police, children of German neighbors who might have denounced a Jewish neighbor, and children of war veterans who may have engaged in unspeakable acts. Phantom memory can also conceal the parents' own homophobia, concealed religious identity, and experiences of child abuse, incest, and murder.[13]

I loved the book by Anne Michaels, *Fugitive Pieces*, and found the film by the same title remarkable. The DVD includes a two-hour commentary by Anne Michaels discussing the entire film. This novel is a restorative narrative of two generations, one who was in the heart of the trauma and the second who was at the edge of it. Their challenges are difficult but for different reasons and require different processing. In the book, the main character, Jakob Beer, suffers from a life-long anguish that can be described as a phantom memory. It begins with Jakob, hiding in a wall of his home, as he watches his parents killed and his sister abducted by Nazi soldiers, never to be seen again. He never knows what happened to his sister and is haunted by that not knowing. There is no possibility that any of his family can receive proper burial; they are entombed, unappeased, within Jakob himself. Dreams plague Jakob Beer until his traumatic past takes over his present.[14]

The film's ending has been changed from that in the book. In the new ending, Jakob Beer's sister comes to him in a visitation and shows him that he can let her go. He realizes that it is as painful for the ghosts to be remembered as it is for him to remember them and that he needs to release her. Anne Michaels appreciates this change in the film, commenting on the DVD: "He has reached a point where he is ready to be seen." Jakob Beer can accept the memories that haunt him and can transcend them, and be seen at last in the sense that he can at last connect with others. His realization, in the words of Anne Michaels, is that "To remain with the dead is to abandon them." That doesn't mean we forget. However, we do have the right to move forward and reclaim our right to live.

In one of my dialogues, Sylvia, a participant, talked about a granddaughter, a twin, who seems to have a type of phantom memory. This is what she described after I related the story of how I experience an inherited memory in my back:

"I think there is a connection, almost a genetic connection. I have twin granddaughters who are ten. They are voracious readers. Sophie is very sensitive. After reading a story that she found in the library, she became obsessed with the Holocaust, so much so that she can't sleep. She has horrific pictures in her mind. I was talking to her today when we went kayaking, and I asked her exactly what she is feeling because I can see this child is suffering. So she talked about the story she read of a fourteen-year-old girl waiting in line during a selection when a man told her to say she was seventeen so she wouldn't go to the gas chamber. She saw her mother and her sister being led away in the other line and never saw then again. Sophie said, "I don't know why I identify with this girl so much." The other twin doesn't express this. Sophie goes out of her way to make sure that I'm not suffering. She wants to know everything about the Holocaust to the extent that it is almost eerie. She's not a particularly vulnerable child; she is very well adjusted, but she is in pain. She is internalizing the lost children."

Decades after the brutal killing of her tribe, Mary Crow Dog, a Lakota woman who coined the phrase *historical trauma*, spoke of her nightmares about these slaughters as though she were experiencing a phantom memory: "In my dream I had been going back into another life. I saw tipis and Indians camping . . . and then, suddenly, I saw white soldiers riding into camp, killing women and children, raping, cutting throats. It was so real . . . sights I did not want to see, but had to see against my will; the screaming of children that I did not want to hear . . . And the only thing I could do was cry . . . For a long time after that dream, I felt depressed, as if all life had been drained from me."[15]

By staying open to the possibility of what we can learn from various forms of memory, we may find information that has not been given a direct voice. Take for example this poem I wrote when I was sixteen. It has no title.

Long shadow
On my short tomb
Still
Beats the heart
Flies to the one-eyed moon
Why
The warriors weep below

I have always been reluctant to dissect the poem. Years later, it is interesting to ask: What or who is the shadow? Why is the word "still" in the middle of the poem? Is the heart still in that it no longer beats, or is it still beating after death? Can it also be that the heart still beats in a new generation? And is the last line a question asking why the warriors are weeping if the heart is still beating, or is it a statement about the ongoing sorrow of the living left below?

Diasporic Memory

The Vietnamese people continue to deal with their inherited trauma. My colleague, Quynh-Tram Nguyen, sent me a piece she wrote about her exploration of the Vietnamese post-war memory, which she calls *diasporic memory*. Diaspora is the dispersion of a people from their homeland. Quynh-Tram considers that diasporic memory links the haunting from loss and dispersion to historical trauma. Her insights are enlightening:

> "Like other displaced groups in the world, the Vietnamese have been forced to face a loss of a life-world and other related necessities to nourish their communal soul in exile. The post-war memory is all that remains, collective in spirit but fragmented in sight. Vietnamese post-war memory engages with past/present relations. Being a lived history rather than "true" history, it is history but not time bound. In addition, it is central in the debate on "the right to remember, the responsibility to recall," and the "sense of the dangers involved in forgetting" their history. It is manifested, modified, and invented from the historical and subjugated knowledge, the difficult knowledge that haunts the Vietnamese Americans of three generations who have experienced, both consciously and unconsciously, colonial wounds and paradoxes of loss and creativity."

Jesse Thistle, a Métis-Cree from Saskatchewan, is studying trauma and memory within the Métis and Cree people of Northern Saskatchewan and the northern Great Plains. In his research, Thistle found out about the dispersal of Métis people after the soldiers attacked Batoche. He learned that his grandmother and uncle fled to Whitefish Reserve in northern Saskatchewan, where they hid for five years, and some of the children they took with them starved to death. The information he found helped him to forgive his parents and understand his ancestors.

"When I returned this history to my family out west, there's been an almost immediate healing. ... Knowing what happened, people can heal from that. When you're undiagnosed, you can't really fight against that. So that keeps me going, the healing that I see from it."[16]

Absent Memory, Post-Memory, Photographs and Art as Memory

The past is never dead. It's not even past.
—William Faulkner, *Go Down Moses*

When we speak of memory, we usually speak of it as reminiscences of a known past; however, as we have seen, memory work can also be about our unknown past or even about someone else's past. Often, the very uncertainty of the past can shape our identities.

Henri Raczymow talks about *absent memory* as gaps in genealogies that leave Inheritors in the position of orphans, feeling excluded and without real roots. Both Hirsch and Raczymow believe that because we are orphans of that world, it must be preserved and mourned but not forgotten. Hirsch quotes Raczymow:

"If the earth is turning to the right, I must turn left in order to catch up with the past . . . European Jews of the postwar generation are forever turning left, but we can never catch up with the past; inasmuch as we remember, we remain perpetual temporal and spatial exiles . . . Our past is literally a foreign country we can never hope to visit. And our absent memory is shaped by our sense of belatedness and disconnection. I neither emigrated nor was deported. The world that was destroyed was not mine. I never knew it. But I am, as so many of us are, the orphans of that world."[17]

Hirsch connects *post memory* with photographs: "Photographs are connections to a lost past, and because many photographic images have survived even though their subjects did not, photographs provide a particularly powerful medium of *post-memory*."[18]

Having photographs, or not having them, came up often in our dialogues. I have a handful of photographs, including a picture of my paternal grandmother and one of my maternal grandparents, as well as a few pictures of my father, and, of course, the cherished picture of my brother, my sister, and their mother. When I hear fellow Inheritors exclaim that they have no pictures, I view this to be an additional calamity.

I feel strongly that one of my roles is to act as a conduit for my family's memory. While my children were growing up, I was the photographer; I created the photo albums that hold the chronological family history, the key holder of their childhood information. My daughter, Natalie, has a habit of looking at the old albums whenever she visits. I think she is finding her place, her identity in relation to me, her mother, to her father and to her own history. The digital age puts me in a quandary about archiving and preserving photographs. For me, "hard copies" of pictures evoke a sense of comfort and safety; I like the feel of their age and even their faded imperfections. I place them securely in photo albums and not in a cloud on the world wide web. Given my history of loss, I very likely do this as an unconscious effort to evade the unexpected event that might eradicate all these memories.

Films, as well as photographs, stir up our memories and touch our senses. They are strong triggers for forms of deep memory that encompass our universal consciousness, like the archetypal images described by Jung. Much of what we think we know about the two World Wars, the wars in Vietnam, Afghanistan, Rwanda, etc., comes from literature and film, or "moving pictures," rather than from historical accounts. We all readily recognize the common constructs in films, such as the soldier in the trenches who provides encouraging tenderness to a fellow soldier, the painful contacts between the nurses and wounded soldiers, and the dying kiss as an act of support and comfort.[19]

Visual art is another media that can speak to us in numerous ways. Marij Bouwmans, who is an artist and a psychotherapist, created a work titled, *Pricking and Threading: Deficits, Defects and Re-pair, a Metaphorical Exploration of Skin*, which deals with her early childhood memories through a metaphorical exploration of skin. Her work consists of children's clothing, hand-stitched clumsily in bright red thread, like something a child would make. She gives us an interesting description of her process and how the art reflects the scars of childhood as well as serving as a medium for finding what has been hidden.

"My work as an artist always begins in an emotional memory. My series of baby and children's clothes are made of latex, a material used to make artificial skin used in the film industry as special effects. The psychological theme of "second skin" is well researched and described in psychoanalytical narrative. Simply said it is a description of the psychological adjustments we make when we, as very young children, are faced with good and less good experiences. How we are spoken to, how and if we are being touched, how we are comforted and mirrored. In short, whether and how, and how much we are loved or not. These adjustments become part of our character and social identity. They become a fingerprint. Sometimes we suffer from it later in life because those adjustments that served us well can get in the way when we form adult intimate relationships . . . This light box of skin shows all sorts of skin scars, hardened pieces and vulnerabilities and holes. Deep under the children's clothes, deep under the skin, there is something hidden."

Our memory work, as per the title of this work by Marij Bouwmans, is like *pricking* and *threading*, or stitching together, the *deficits* and *defects* of our life's experience. The act of creating the art piece serves to uncover that which is suppressed or hidden as a shield to cover the wounds. This stitching process continues over a lifetime as we experience new cuts.

Alice Miller, a psychiatrist whose book, *The Drama of the Gifted Child*, opened me up to the perpetuating generational aspects of family dysfunction, says that the suppressed experience for the purpose of self protection is not easily uncovered because the individual may not know what they have hidden, making it exponentially more difficult to access that "inner prison" and bring it to the conscious mind.

> The company of prison wardens does not encourage lively development. It is only after it is liberated in analysis that the self begins to articulate, to grow, and to develop its creativity. Where there had only been fearful emptiness or equally frightening grandiose fantasies, there now is unfolding an unexpected wealth of vitality. This is not a homecoming since this home had never before existed. It is the discovery of home."[20]

I don't agree that it is only in analysis that the Self can be liberated. I will be talking about dialogue, the arts, and the meaning we create from our relationships as other forms of release from the cage. But the concept is important as expressed by one of her patients. I've presented it like a poem, the last line of which evokes a powerful image that speaks volumes about the work of uncovering our unknown layers.

> *I lived in a glass house into which my mother could*
> *look at any time.*
> *In a glass house, however, you cannot conceal*
> *anything without giving yourself away,*
> *except by hiding it under the ground.*
> *And then you cannot see it yourself either.*[21]

Constructing Your Story

Chapter 4 Questions: Different Forms of Memory

- Having read this chapter, how would you answer the question posed at the beginning of the chapter: "Do we carry memory from one generation to another?"

- Have you experienced a light bulb moment—an *a-ha* about something that you knew but didn't realize you knew? Describe this memory or knowledge and what you now know.

- How does this new sense of knowing feel?

5

SPEAKING / NOT-SPEAKING

GLOBAL SILENCE

The opposite of love is not hate, but indifference.

—Elie Wiesel,
Holocaust survivor, international author,
recipient of the Nobel Peace Prize and
the Presidential Medal of Freedom

Sociopolitical Influences

Global silence and cover-ups after catastrophic events are not uncommon, given changing geo-political perspectives, new alliances, and new borders. These forms of silence are mirrored at the individual and personal levels. Certainly this was true after the Holocaust. It has been called the *conspiracy of silence*. After WWII, there were historical and political reasons for a lengthy silence about many aspects of the War and of the Holocaust. Germany was now an ally and the new enemy was Russia; the new war was the Cold War. So the history of the communist resistance to the Germans was officially banned from memory and from books, effectively silencing it.

The political pressure for silence permeated Hollywood as well. US President Roosevelt did not want to demonize Germany, so in 1944, his Office of War wrote a memo to Hollywood producers. They were instructed to ensure that domestic films balance good and bad with a purposeful effort depicting the good. Anti-Semitism was to be dealt with as a social problem and as an aberration (not a normal phenomenon) and as un-American (as in the film *Gentlemen's Agreement*). The events of the Holocaust were mostly seen in newsreels and documentaries. The Holocaust and genocide were not depicted in movies until 1958, with *The Young Lions* and *The Diary of Anne Frank*, followed by *The Pawnbroker* in 1964. Sophie's Choice in 1982 and Schindler's List in 1994 followed these, almost 50 years after the end of the war. Given the influence of movies, this lack certainly created a gap in our society's world-view of the Holocaust and meant there was no permission for survivors to speak about it outside of their communities.

Little Known Heroic Rescues

Information about heroes and their courageous acts in saving Jews were also covered up. Anna Mieszkowska explains this in relation to the relative anonymity of Irena Sendler, a Christian woman who saved 2,500 children in Poland: "In Poland it has always been easier to talk about martyrs than about heroes . . . It is easier to talk about Janusz Korczak [a progressive educator, doctor and director of Christian and Jewish orphanages who chose to go to the gas chambers with his orphans when he was offered his freedom] than about Irena Sendler, because she makes us realize what we have not done but could have done . . . For many years in Poland this was not discussed. It was as if hiding of Jews was a shameful subject."[1]

There were numerous rescues, too many to mention, but many are also not known for a variety of reasons. One of the most famous of rescuers, thanks to the wide dissemination of *The Diary of Anne Frank,* is Miep Gies, the woman who tried to save Anne Frank and her family; her own, most interesting book, *Anne Frank Remembered,* was originally published in 1987. The book's opening quote is from Anne Frank's diary entry, written on May 8, 1944: "It seems as if we are never far from Miep's thoughts . . ."[2]

A different story is that of Anne Frank's best friend, Jacqueline van Maarsen, who was with her until her death. She kept her story silent through most of her life. In an interview with the *Epoch Times,* Maarsen reveals that the girls had met at school in 1941 when they were twelve, and were together in the Bergen Belsen concentration camp. They had been so close that van Maarsen couldn't separate her own memories from those in Anne Frank's diary. For decades, she hid the pain of her Holocaust memories and her friendship with Anne. The only person she spoke to was Otto Frank, Anne's father, who visited the sixteen-year old Maarsen frequently. He cried unabashedly during their talks and he always asked at the end of each conversation: "what would Anne be doing if she were alive today?" Ever since her friend's diary gained international fame, Jacqueline van Maarsen struggled with a dilemma. If she told her story, would she be known only as Anne Frank's best friend for the rest of her life, without an identity of her own? In the late 1980s van Maarsen decided that it was her duty to talk if keeping Anne Frank's memory alive would prevent future genocides. As ethnic cleansing, religious persecution, and genocide continued, she would regularly ask herself whether Anne Frank would want her to tell their story; the answer was always "Yes." Van Maarsen now gives as many interviews as she can in New York and Amsterdam. After all, as Anne Frank wrote in her diary: "In spite of everything I still believe that people are really good at heart."[3]

When Jewish deportations began, many Jews were hidden in Catholic areas. Parish priests created networks for hiding Jews, and unlike the cities, close-knit country parishes were able to hide Jews without being informed upon by neighbours. Martin Gilbert wrote, "As in every country under German occupation, so in Holland, local priests played a major part in rescuing Jews."[4]

An astonishing story that demonstrates the capacities of mankind to help their fellow man comes from the entire country of Albania. In September 1943, Albania came under German control, and in the beginning of 1944, the Germans ordered the Jews to register for eventual deportation. The Albanians, including government officials, helped the Jews to find refuge with Albanian families and with partisans. This small, mostly Muslim country helped save all but two families of Jews. At a photo exhibit I read that Mehdi Frasheri, the Albanian prime minister at the time, declared, "All Jewish children will sleep with your children, all will eat the same food, all will live as one family." The core of this humanity lay in the concept of *besa*, which means "to keep the promise." The promise is a code of honor linked to an Albanian folk principle of taking responsibility for others in their time of need. Because of that code, between eighteen hundred and two thousand Jews were saved in Albania. The stories about the Albanian rescuers are relatively unknown because of the country's political isolation under communism. It wasn't until the late 1980s, at the end of the cold war, that this story came to light.[5]

Another example of a little-known act of rescue occurred in Denmark. The Nazis planned to round up the Danish Jews on Yom Kippur. A member of the German army tipped off the chief rabbi, who immediately sent his community a strange order not to come to the synagogue on the high holiday. Meanwhile, thousands of non-Jews welcomed their Jewish neighbors into their homes. They moved them by night to the east coast, where Danish fishermen rowed them to safety in neighboring Sweden. Over 6,000 Jews were saved in this mass rescue.[6]

On meeting a Japanese journalist, Aya Takahashi, I learned the interesting story of Chiune Sugihara, who is more widely known in Japan than in the rest of the world. Sugihara was a Japanese diplomat assigned to Lithuania in 1939 in order to observe German and Soviet troop movements and to predict the outbreak of the German-Soviet war. In Timothy Snyder's, *The Black Earth*, Snyder details the fascinating account of how Sugihara, together with Michal Rybikowski—who was running an Allied spy network from neutral Sweden, along with two Polish intelligence officers (in exile), Alfons Jakubianec and Leszek Daszkiewicz, and the Dutch honorary consul—developed a complex scheme to prepare an escape route to Japan via Curaçao, an island in the Caribbean Sea and a Dutch colony. They issued about 3,500 visas to Polish citizens, a third of whom were Jews. Since one visa sufficed for a family, some eight thousand Jews left Europe.[7]

There were Jewish heroes who saved lives as well. The largest single revolt by Jews during World War II is known as the Ghetto Uprising of 1943. (It is often confused with the Warsaw Uprising, but the ghetto uprising took place over a year before the Warsaw Uprising of 1944, at which point most of the Jews had been destroyed). In 1943, in an act of futile resistance, ghetto fighters tried to stop the final transport of the last remaining ghetto population to their deaths in Treblinka. The uprising started on 19 April, when the ghetto refused to surrender to the police commander SS-Brigadeführer Jürgen Stroop, who then ordered the burning of the ghetto, block by block. The uprising ended on 16 May. A total of thirteen thousand Jews died, about half of them burnt alive or suffocated. One of my parents' friends somehow survived the Warsaw Ghetto and fought in the uprising. He appeared quite different than my father, more muscular with chiselled features—in other words, like the stereotype of a hero. My son loved him, and he seemed so straightforward in the manner he returned my son's affections. We were all shocked when he attempted to commit suicide by jumping off the third story of his apartment building. I don't know if anyone knew what were the thoughts and visions that haunted him.

Abba Kovner, a poet turned resistance fighter, was from my mother's city of Vilna, and was known by my mother. When he learned that, rather than being transported to labor camps, Jews were being taken to the forests of Ponary to be shot and buried in pits—and having read Hitler's *Mein Kampf*—he decided to write his famous appeal to resist to the last breath. It was a strongly worded speech that included: "Hitler plans to destroy all the Jews of Europe, and the Jews of Lithuania have been chosen as the first in line." One of the lines in the speech has caused much angst: "We will not be led like sheep to the slaughter!" Although it was intended as a rallying cry, after the war many Jews accused the survivors of going to their deaths "like sheep to the slaughter." We will see later that vindication of the survivors came with the Eichmann trial.

Kovner led the Vilna ghetto fighters to their escape through the city's sewers and other outlets to the Rudniky forests, where they joined Soviet partisans and performed many heroic acts of sabotage. A 1986 documentary, *The Partisans of Vilna,* provides much insight into the situation and the resistance. Claude Lanzmann's interviews with Kovner provides further insight on Kovner's role in rallying resistance against the coming slaughter.[8]

The 2008 film, *Defiance,* depicts the true story of the Bielski brothers. After their family was killed, they became the leaders of partisan fighters in the forests of Belarus. They accepted anyone who came to their encampment, built a village, and saved over one thousand Jewish non-combatants. The parents of one of the dialogue participants fought with the Bielski partisans. Sylvia tells the story of her parents' tragic sacrifice and of their unbelievable escape from the ghetto into the woods where the partisans were camped.

SYLVIA: My parents were in the ghetto. The inhabitants planned their escape by building a tunnel over a six-month period. It ran a kilometer in length and had electricity with light bulbs. They would carry two bags in and carry two bags out with earth every day. The plan was that in the fall, when the corn was high, they would escape. In the meantime, the Bielski partisans were in the woods. In the fall, they tied themselves together and got ready to leave. My father was out on a detail. They needed to keep the children quiet, and my mother, who was a nurse, euthanized the children including their own small child.

KATHI: I thought they euthanized them accidentally! Your mother never got over it.

SYLVIA: No, she didn't.

EVERYONE: How old was your little brother?

SYLVIA: One cousin told me the child was 6 months, another that he was 3 months. After their escape they joined the Bielski partisans in the forest.

GITA: Did any of your family talk about memories of this time?

SYLVIA: Nobody talked about it. There were a lot of untouchable topics.

ABIGAIL: There were a lot of untouchable topics.

A wrenching example of quiet, noble heroism is the story of Janusz Korczak, a children's author, pedagogist, and famous paediatrician in Poland. After spending many years as a director of both

Jewish and Christian orphanages, he was offered freedom when the order came to liquidate the Jewish children, but he refused and instead stayed with the Jewish orphans when they were sent to extermination camps. On August 5, 1942, weakened by fatigue and undernourishment, Korscak walked with his head held high, leading his two hundred children in calm, orderly ranks through the hushed streets of Warsaw to the train station. They carried the orphanage flag that Korczak had designed—green with white blossoms on one side and the blue Star of David on the other. This is how Joshua Perle, an eyewitness, described the procession of Korczak and the children through the ghetto to the *Umschlagplatz* (deportation point to the death camps):

> "The children were dressed in their best clothes, and each carried a blue knapsack and a favorite book or toy. They walked in lines of four with Korczak at their head. This was not a march off to cattle cars, but a silent, disciplined protest against murder . . . A miracle occurred. Two hundred children did not cry out. Two hundred pure souls, condemned to death, did not weep. Not one of them ran away. No one tried to hide. Like stricken swallows they clung to their teacher and mentor, to their father and brother, Janusz Korczak, so that he might protect and preserve them. Janusz Korczak was marching his head bent forward, without a hat, a leather belt around his waist, and wearing high boots, holding the hand of a child. A few nurses were followed by two hundred children dressed in clean and meticulously cared for clothes, as if they were being carried to the altar. On all sides the children were surrounded by Germans, Ukrainians, and also Jewish Ghetto Police. They whipped them and shots were fired at them. The very stones of the street wept at the sight of the procession. According to a popular legend, when the group of orphans finally reached the *Umschlagplatz* an SS officer recognized Korczak as the author of one of his favorite children's books and offered to

help him escape. By another version, the officer was acting officially, as the Nazi authorities had in mind some kind of *special treatment* for Korczak. Whatever the offer, Korczak once again refused. He boarded the trains with the children and was never heard from again."[9]

I must mention one of my father's heroes, Arthur Zygielbaum. In Montreal, my father belonged to an organization called "The Worker's Circle." My father's Chapter was named after Ziegelbaum, who set himself on fire on the streets of London to protest the lack of reaction from the Allied governments and the world in general. In his farewell note, he wrote: "I cannot continue to live and to be silent while the remnants of Polish Jewry, whose representative I am, are being murdered . . . By my death, I wish to give expression to my most profound protest against the inaction in which the world watches and permits the destruction of the Jewish people."[10]

Young children also played heroic roles. In 1941 the official daily food rations distributed on the basis of ration cards were allocated by the Nazis according to the following ethnically differentiated scale: the Germans were allotted 2,613 calories per day, the Poles 669, while persons of Jewish origin were allowed only 184 calories a day, a diet insufficient for survival. Consequently, in the Warsaw Ghetto fully eighty percent of all food consumed had to be smuggled in as illicit contraband. Children, because of their small size, were able to slither undetected through small openings and sewer lines on their way to and from the Ghetto. These child heroes saved or prolonged the lives of countless adult individuals, but they themselves fell victim in large numbers to the bullets of German police. This poem, *Mały szmugler/The Little Smuggler*, reflects the motivation and risks taken by those young children.

The Little Smuggler

Through a hole, through a cranny,
Starving yet stubborn and canny,
Sneaking and speedy like a cat
I daily risk my youthful neck.
And if faith will turn against me,
In that game of life and bread,
Do not weep for me, Mother, do not cry,
Are we not all marked to die?

Only one worry besets me,
Laying in agony, so near death,
Who will care for you, tomorrow,
Who will bring you, dear Mom
A slice of bread.

The author of the poem, Henryka Łazowertówna, together with her mother, Bluma Łazowertowa, was killed in the gas chambers of the Treblinka extermination camp.[11]

Silenced Information

There is information that we want to know, and then there is some information that is hard to hear and we may not want to know. Information on medical torture, for example, is impossible for most of us to read, yet many scholars are now discovering multiple references to Nazi experiments republished in reputable medical literature. These studies and references frequently bear no disclaimer as to how the data was obtained. In recent years, several scientists who have sought to use Nazi research have stirred widespread soul-searching about the social responsibility and potential abuses of science.

Some information that is generally not known, but important to know, is that of policies for the forced sterilization and murder of disabled persons, including people diagnosed with schizophrenia, epilepsy, so-called feeblemindedness, hereditary blindness, severe hereditary physical deformity, severe alcoholism, and other ailments. These policies began in the 1930s, many years before the Holocaust, and continued with force during the Holocaust. This information has been exposed in a poignantly-titled book, *Crying Hands,* by Horst Biesold.[12] It is important that we stay vigilant to the dangers of concepts such as "eugenics" that promote human genetic manipulation and which are important markers of potential ethnic cleansing. It is a policy familiar to African Americans.

The recent publication of a book of essays edited by Sonja Hedgepeth, with the telling title, *Sexual Violence Against Jewish Women During the Holocaust,* has met with much angst. The interdisciplinary anthology touches on everything from rape, forced prostitution, sterilizations and abortion, to psychological trauma, gender-identity issues, and depictions of violence in the art of Jewish and non-Jewish women. It is believed to be the first book in English to focus exclusively on this subject. One of the essays, *The Tragic Fate of Ukrainian Women under Nazi Occupation 1941–1944,* by Russian author Anatoly Podolsky, was likely only made possible as a result of a newly-opened archives in Russia held by the former Soviet Union. Gloria Steinem reviewed Hedgepeth's book and speculated, "Perhaps we would have been better able to prevent the rapes in the former Yugoslavia and the Congo if we had not had to wait more than 60 years to hear the truths that are anthologized in *Sexual Violence against Jewish Women during the Holocaust.*"[13] As a result of this book, Steinem was inspired to create the project, *Women Under Siege.*

Paula David, a professor of gerontology at the University of Toronto, has worked for twenty years with Holocaust survivors as they enter their final years. David heard stories about sexual violence slip through their lips as they lost their ability to self-censor or to consciously choose what they shared. She would hear things like, "It wasn't sex; it was bread." These older women have helped reveal the long-held secrets of sexual trauma.[14]

The story of "comfort women," a euphemism for the sex slaves who served the Japanese Armed Forces, has only recently come to light. Women from Japan, Korea, China, the Dutch East Indies, Burma, and elsewhere were kidnapped, or lured by promises of work only to end up working as sex slaves. Estimates of their numbers vary from twenty thousand to four hundred thousand.[15]

Had the world listened to stories such as these, information about sexual violence might have come to light earlier. As it was, the United Nations did not declare rape a war crime until 2008, with Resolution 1820. Unfortunately, this legal requirement did not help in Rwanda in 1994, when between 250,000 and 500,000 women were raped during 100 days of genocide. Up to 20,000 children were born to Rwandan women as a result of rape. More than 67 percent of women who were raped were also infected with HIV and AIDS. In many cases, this resulted from a systematic and planned use of rape by HIV-positive men as a weapon of genocide.[16]

A final example deals with previously unavailable archived documentation detailing records that had been kept by the Nazis. In 1955, the Allies created the International Tracing Service (ITS), an arm of the International Committee of the Red Cross, which was put in charge of the archives to help repatriate people displaced by World War II. These records—50 million pages on 16 miles of shelves in six buildings in the small German town of Bad Arolsen—detailed the fates of all 17.5 million Holocaust victims, including forced and slave laborers, and displaced persons (DPs) of many ethnic groups. This archive contains the famous "Schindler's List" and records of Anne Frank's journey from Amsterdam to Bergen-Belsen. However, the ITS considered these records "personal information" and access to them was severely restricted. This meant that the collective evidence offered by the archive's thirty million documents was not available to historians, academics, or survivors. In 2007, masses of important documents were released, thanks to the efforts of Paul Shapiro, Director of the Center for Advanced Holocaust Studies at the US Holocaust Memorial Museum. Some information is still not accessible, including victimization records, information on property and possessions, slave labor information, Nazi records, information held by the United Nations on war crimes, and information held by the Vatican.[17] It seems incredible that so much information has remained hidden and inaccessible for almost seventy years, since the end of World War II. What is also difficult to bear is the irretrievable information that has been lost on the culture and life of our Jewish ancestors.

Constructing Your Story

Questions for Chapter 5:
Speaking/Not Speaking: Global Silence

- In your political and historical life context, what information has not been made known or fully acknowledged?

- Are you the type of person who needs to know, or would you rather put it behind you? Why?

6

SPEAKING / NOT-SPEAKING

FAMILY SILENCE

My mother talked, but my father didn't.
My father talked, but not my mother.
We didn't talk about it at home.
We talked about it all the time.

—Spoken by Inheritors everywhere.

Survivor and Inheritor Perspectives

They couldn't take it, because to be a survivor is not easy in a world that doesn't want to listen. And to be a child of survivors is equally difficult in a world that doesn't want to remember.

—Elie Wiesel

The issue of global silence has direct impact on silence in families. The survivor parents and grandparents often withheld information about the ordeals of the past. There are a variety of reasons for this, but I found very helpful an insight made by a veteran of Afghanistan who is suffering from PTSD and who is also both a grandson of a veteran of World War I and the son of a veteran of World War II. He was interviewed in a 2015 CBC documentary, *When the Boys Come Home*. This is how the veteran explains *not-speaking*.

"Dad told me he never wanted to talk about it. Growing up I always wondered: 'why don't you want to talk about it? You're a hero, you were overseas, you fought a war, you fought for your country?' Now I know why they didn't speak because it was horrible and you want to forget about it, and the more you talk about it, the more you remember. If you just stop talking about it, maybe you'll forget, and if you forget, maybe you'll stop the nightmares."

There were many reasons for parents to not speak. My father is an example of a man who didn't speak because, as I now understand, he was plagued by the loss of his family and also by his guilt for leaving them. Once in a while, he would briefly lament, "I had two families!" But before he died, my father asked me, "Do you think I am a good man?" I knew what he meant, and assured him he was a good man. I doubt that my assurance was enough.

Many parents wanted to shelter their children from the horrors and the burdens of the past and the guilt and shame that it often carries. Judith Maier, a dialogue participant, described learning about her parents' experience for the firt time, when they gave evidence at a trial of a Nazi officer:

> "My father spoke to me only at the time of the 1965 trial when he gave evidence for the trial of Handke, an officer, and of Movinkel, the commander of the LIPOWA 7 Camp in Lublin. It was a turning point in my life, because on the one hand, they didn't want to tell me about it; on the other hand, I saw the sadness when they were talking about it. When they noticed me coming, they would say: 'shah, dos kiend / shh, the child.' Plus their shouting at night was traumatizing. Both of them were shouting like animals. They always said it was a bad dream. When police officers came to take evidence, I was fifteen, just coming home from school and I listened. The evidence started with my father. When I understood about their life, it was a release."

The following conversation is about what parents did or did not tell, and how we knew regardless. It ends with a surprising discovery of similarities among us.

LEAH: My mother told me a little about her family but not my father. I don't even know the names of my half-brothers.

GITA: I'm on a quest to find out about my half-brother and sister.

PNINA: My father never talked about his wife and children. We somehow knew.

ESTHER: How did you know?

PNINA: Because a child always knows. There was a picture of a woman and two children. When we asked about them, they just said someone in the family.

ESTHER: How old were the children?

PNINA: Four and three.

GITA (a little shocked at the similarity of ages to that of my siblings): My siblings were exactly the same, four and three. I'll show you their picture.

ESTHER: [looking at the picture] Wow!

LEAH: My father had been very religious, but changed—he said the Shoah finished it, there is no God.

PNINA: I'm not religious.

GITA: I'm not religious.

ESTHER: I'm not religious.

For some Inheritors, the family secrets had a normalizing effect. Itzik, a dialogue partici-pant, told the group that he had a happy childhood:

ITZIK: My parents are from Czechoslovakia and came in 1949. My father was in Auschwitz at age nineteen and my mother was also in Auschwitz at age fifteen. My father spoke a little. I know it was hell. My mother didn't talk at all. My father had experiments done on him—they took out his appendix without anaesthetic. He tried to escape, was shot, was beaten. I don't know what happened to their families.

ESTHER: There are records, you can do research.

ITZIK: I don't know if I want to. I don't know when I first heard. But my childhood was great. My parents love each other to this day. I had a fairy-tale life; I was not over-protected. My mother would have seen and experienced terrible things: Mengele saying, you go here, you go there. (Mengele was a doctor in Auschwitz who performed horrific medical experiments.) How could she talk about it if it can't be explained or understood. I did tell my children and gave them the freedom to ask their grandparents questions if they wanted to.

So we can see the desire for parents to shelter their children while the children feared creating more hurt or guilt for their parents. Certainly asking a question was no simple matter and because we didn't ask the questions, we are left with many gaps in information.

Young children, also by necessity, couldn't ask questions and found other strategies to cope and protect themselves in the only way a child can. I well remember an incident when I needed to escape the Holocaust; I could not take hearing these stories of horrific deaths and tragic losses. I did speak up and drew the line. I was very young and had been in Canada for only about two years. My father would often take me to Yiddish/Jewish-language films; some were about the Holocaust and some were amusing and silly. My mother wouldn't go, my brother was too young. I wanted to be grateful for my father's good efforts, knowing how hard it was for him to speak and connect, and it was so nice for just the two of us to be together without my interfering mother to spoil things. But some of those films were frightening, too emotionally advanced for a child of about six or seven years old. There was one film in particular that was too much for me. It began with a scene of a family, an older brother and his parents who, when they heard the Nazis coming, hid their beloved little girl, who wore a beautiful white dress. The Nazis found her in the chest where she was hidden, and brutally threw this lovely child down the stairs. I am still haunted by this image. I told my father I would not go to these movies anymore, but I was too young to be capable of telling him that it was too overwhelming for me to handle. I have always felt guilty for abandoning him and our time together.

I used to believe that our family did talk about the Holocaust. Sure, I knew there was little coherence in my parents' stories and that there were gaps in the information I received, but I only now realize how big those gaps actually were. It has been gratifying to hear that others had the same experience, as captured in this dialogue:

YOSSI: My mother never told her whole story; it was full of holes. They'll never tell you the whole story; they'll suppress it, tell you parts but not other parts. Some people appear that they never mentioned and disappear the next time you ask. The story is full of holes.

GITA: Yes, my mother was with her brother the whole time she was running, but I never got that; she somehow neglected to mention it.

YOSSI: We don't have continuity; we don't have a past.

DOUBI: We don't have a *complete* past.

YOSSI: No, we don't have a past. We came to Israel from a place from which we have no memories, no pictures, no albums, no stories.

ESTHER: We don't have roots.

DOUBI: I have pictures from before the war.

YOSSI: I have one picture that was sent to the US and we got a copy of that one picture.

ITZIK: My father has pictures; my mother has nothing. Regarding roots, we know nothing about the last five, eight generations.

This poem that I wrote describes the collusion of silence, between our parents and ourselves, to not necessarily talk about things we really don't want to talk about or hear.

I Haven't Been Listening

I haven't been listening
To what you haven't been saying
I haven't wanted to hear
What you haven't wanted to say

Words left unspoken
Melt into nothing
Melting hope
Melting joy
Melting peace

It's really a sad and empty thing
When words don't belong anywhere

Because they've been left unsaid
When arms remain empty
Because they can hold no truth
When love is in turmoil
Because it doesn't have a place to rest

And time is in limbo
Always waiting, always waiting, always waiting
Because

The effect of global and family silence on Inheritors is that they not only remain silent themselves, but that they also absorb the guilt, the fear, the shame, and the helplessness of previous generations, without having any direct access to those experiences or even to a meaningful frame of reference. The next poem reveals how I bore my trials silently and, like my parents, was hyper-vigilant and reactive to authority, as I looked out at the unstable world, unable to know what face to put on for it. (I should add I have hopefully moved on from this uncomfortable way of being.)

Posture

I keep my head
Sticking out from my neck
Like someone expecting
To have it chopped off

I keep my head
Sticking out from my neck
Like someone on the alert
To oncoming danger

I keep my head bowed
Like a humble monk
Not knowing what face

To project to the world

I would like to take my head
In my hands
Like Ichabod Crane
And put it back
Straight

So no one would know
What really goes on
In my misaligned
Self
So no one would know
I was so scared and unsure.

The Canadian Indigenous community also faces the challenge of family silence. Many of their grandmothers and grandfathers who suffered physical, mental, emotional, and sexual abuse in Residential Schools do not want to speak about it. Their descendants are reaching out to them, urging them to speak. It is a familiar scenario: the parents do not speak, and the children need to understand the story behind the void that they have inherited. With the aging of survivor parents age, the cry for information becomes more desperate. Interestingly, for both Jewish and Indigenous survivors, their parents are more likely to speak to their grandchildren than to their children.

The African American inheritors also share the experience of family secrets, given the racial traumas that they wanted to shield from their children: "At times, it has required considerable effort and much persuasion to retrieve the missing pieces of a traumatic event in the family history. In some families, the fates of the murdered persons are withheld from the younger generation to protect them from painful stories."[1]

Harriet Lerner describes the child rescuer who, in order to rescue their parents from having to deal with their own issues, will under-function, e.g. underperform in school or get into trouble, so that their parents are spared dealing with their own issues but instead use the distraction to move their attention to the *bad* child. The trajectory of this behavior is that the child becomes an unhealthy adult who gets into trouble.[2]

Alice Miller also speaks of the child as rescuer, and was one of the first to explain the generational perpetuation of family trauma or dysfunction. In her seminal book, *The Drama of the Gifted Child*, what she means by "gifted child" is the sensitive child who sublimates their needs for the needs of their parents. She says that usually a family has such a child, a rescuer of the parents. The result is that the child is left with a void, since his or her own needs are not being met. This creates a multi-generational cycle of repressed pain, which is perpetuated as each subsequent generation fills the void of their parents, creating a void within themselves which then demands to be filled by their children, and so on and so on. "Every mother carries with her a bit of her *unmastered past*, which she unconsciously hands to her child . . . [because] children are intelligent, alert, attentive, extremely sensitive and because they are completely attuned to her well-being, . . . and because they are transparent, clear, reliable and easy to manipulate . . . they are at their parents' disposal and ready for their use."[3] Alice Miller aimed to teach parents to stop making their children take on their problems, stories, dramas, or emotional needs. Rather, the parental role should be to acknowledge and validate their children's emotions without interference by their own emotions. To deny the child this validation is to deny their sense of self within society, and this leaves the child with a sense of isolation. A lack of validation can lead to experiences of "depression" with an accompanying sense of emptiness, futility, fear of impoverishment, loneliness, shame, and anger. (Chapter Eleven speaks about validation in further detail).

What Miller has recognized is that it is the tragic loss of the Self in childhood that manifests as a sense of alienation or emptiness in the adult. The adult, though seemingly successful, cannot fill the old gap, the wound of the child. (We will talk about her counsel on what we can do to heal that wound in the next section on "Unresolved Grief and Mourning.")

In the case of *Inheritor* Indigenous children, because their parents were children when they were taken to Residential Schools, they themselves did not experience being parented. As a result, many survivors and Inheritors were unable to fully take on the parental role. Since this traumatization has been taking place for over seven or eight generations, we are faced with a self-perpetuating problem. Of course, the Inheritor children have no way of understanding this, and without the safety and comfort of their parents' care, the underlying cause of high rates of addictions, drug and alcohol abuse may be their way of self-soothing. And because seven or eight generations have now have gone through the Residential Schools, the welfare system, and the foster care system, the impact of this kind of trauma is cumulative and will continue to be so if it isn't addressed with unrelenting focus. Currently the Indigenous community has the highest rate of suicide rates of any culturally identifiable group in the world. This is a crisis that is happening now!

To summarize this discussion, the danger of silence, whether it is intentional or unconscious, whether it originates in the socio-political environment or in the family—is that it is transformed into an unintentional silencing of the child, leaving the child without an identity of their own and without a sense of the validity of their own emotions. Further, the ramifications of the historical gaps, the wounds of the child and of the parent, are then passed on to future generations, creating a perpetual cycle of unknown and unacknowledged trauma and dysfunction.

Unresolved Grief and Mourning

I saw grief drinking a cup of sorrow and called out, "It tastes sweet, does it not?" "You've caught me," grief answered, "and you've ruined my business. How can I sell sorrow, when you know it's a blessing?"

—Rumi

As we have seen, after the war a new political world existed where the enemy, Germany, had become an ally. A "cold war" with Russia was setting in, and a new social order emerged whereby people from all sides just hunkered down and quietly got on with their lives. Suddenly, survivors of Treblinka could be seen strolling the avenues in Europe, holding a new baby in their arms, showing no signs of recent hunger and forced marches. Within a matter of years, they went from freedom and prosperity to near starvation and death, and back again. Despite multiple traumas—imprisonment, physical hardship, humiliation, and more (referred to as *sequential traumatization*) —still there was no wish to discuss the horrors of war. People just wanted to move on—but in doing so, it was as if they had lost their voice. I would say our parents got on with life, but not in a real way. They developed various unconscious coping strategies. Some of these strategies worked; many did not. A form of melancholia certainly surrounded them and haunted us. I won't call this *depression*, because it doesn't originate from a mental illness.

There were no support vehicles, no trauma counselling to enable individuals to speak of their pain and horrific experiences, and there were no accepted ways to grieve and mourn. My parents and most of their friends lost their faith, which meant that religious avenues of solace were not available to many of them. It is not surprising that survivors faced difficulties in resolving their grief. I wonder at my father's brave silent suffering. He never had the opportunity to mourn the death of his wife and two children. I regret that I had not given him more comfort than I did. I regret that I did not give him the honor he deserved for his bravery.

The impact of unresolved mourning, known as *aberrated mourning*, provides an explanation of why the pain haunts the descendants of these survivors. When the mourner does not or cannot grieve, they become locked in their own trauma, unable to work through it. The opposite occurs in inaugurated mourning, when the grief comes out into the open necessary for the person to be ready to go on with life in a real way. Dan Bar-On found in his studies of loss and trauma that the impact on the child Inheritor shows a consistent relation between unresolved or *aberrated* mourning and the child's successful coping; it is not the trauma itself but the lack of resolution of mourning that creates difficulties for the child, who perceives the parent as either frightened or directly frightening.[4]

Further, Alice Miller counsels us that our wounds cannot be healed without the mourning of what our inner child has missed at critical times. She says that the greatest of narcissist wounds is not to have been loved just as one truly was. Alice Miller draws our attention to the need for us to be aware when we find ourselves repeating a trauma. She says that the work of mourning is required to make up for the lack of understanding; otherwise, we are bound to repeat the trauma, or cover it up in grandiosity or depression.[5]

Repetition compulsion is a psychoanalytic concept developed by Sigmund Freud. It is pertinent here because it is about the compulsion to repeat a traumatic event over and over again. I prefer to call this phenomenon *repetitive trauma,* simply because it is easier to remember and the meaning is more transparent. An example of repetitive trauma is when a person repeatedly re-enacts a traumatic event or has dreams and flashbacks of the event. It also describes a person who repeats the same distressing behaviors that have not served them but have become life patterns. A common repetition trauma is when one continuously chooses a partner who doesn't love you or re-enacting a hurtful episode.

I have coached people who repeat the story of an incident that happened many years ago over and over again. Becoming aware of the pattern is the first step to breaking the pattern. The second step is to make up for the hurt by validating and loving yourself. One can do that for oneself without a psychiatrist. I have framed and put up pictures of myself at various ages (it may look vain but it is for a good cause). I often look at this child and love her and validate her sadness. When I am beating up on myself, I look at her and she reminds me that I should not inflict any more wounds on myself than what I have had already. She helps me with her love.

Dina Wardi relates Inheritor sadness to that of the survivors' inability to mourn. "Survivors seem immersed in mourning, but it is not a real mourning; rather, it is a depressive state resembling mourning only in its external manifestations. A normal mourning process leads to identification with the lost object along with increasing emotional liberation from it, restoring the equilibrium in the mourner's psyche . . . [The loss is] an open wound in the soul of the survivor parent and he/she transmits the burden of that pain to the Inheritor generation; it is only when the Inheritor child becomes an adult that they can be helped."[6]

Perhaps my compulsion to carry out the task of finding documents about the death of my siblings is a way to compensate for an inability to mourn them. I recently added their names to my father's tombstone as a way to make them real. It hit home that I did not know the dates of either their births or deaths, but I was relieved that I found a way to memorialize them.

It seems plausible that aberrated mourning continues from one generation to another if the feelings of grief are not supported and validated as real and worthy. Where there should have been rituals of mourning, there were none. There was only silence. There was only the unspeakable and the invisible, destroyed past. As per our earlier discussion on phantom memory, the result of aberrated mourning is that the dead are encrypted within subsequent generations.

As you will see in the next chapter, on the *Inheritor Syndrome,* our emotions were intolerable to our parents, and even if we could talk to them, we didn't feel we could add to their burdens. As children, we needed to escape the intolerable story we inherited, and so we got on with our lives without talking about the emptiness sitting at our cores. We know from the mind-body-spirit movement that it is important to be aware of and to express our *feelings, thoughts,* and *wants.* We also know from the lessons of global silence that silence and inaction are not options when people are being victimized and violated. The next discussion offers some thoughts that might be helpful for those who wish to end the perpetuation of loss and pain for future generations.

Constructing Your Story

Questions for Chapter 6:
Speaking, Not Speaking: Family Silence

- In your family context, what information has not been made known or fully acknowledged?

- What do you think are the effects on you of these family secrets?

- What have your parents mourned which they were unable to voice adequately?

- What have you (not your parents) been grieving which you have been unable to voice adequately?

- How can recognizing your unacknowledged grief make a difference in your path towards reclaiming your life?

- Take some time to think about recurring patterns in your life that are not serving you. Could you be repeating a trauma pattern that you are used to? How can an awareness of repetitive trauma patterns help you?

7

THE INHERITOR SYNDROME

*I've been searching for something
taken out of my soul
Something I would never lose
Something somebody stole . . .*

—Billy Joel,
River of Dreams

To recap our discussion so far: there are a range of catastrophic events that our ancestors may have suffered, including displacement, killings, starvation, forced slavery, internment in POW camps, forced migration, environmental disasters, economic disasters, victimization, racism, religious persecution, and physical, emotional, and sexual abuse. As a result of these experiences, many of the survivors have suffered from a type of disorder now commonly referred to as Post-Traumatic Stress Disorder, or simply as PTSD. PTSD can manifest as dysfunctional relationships, mental and physical health issues, addictions, severe depression and suicide, anxiety, and other challenges. Inheritors may have experienced the second-hand effects of their traumatized families and communities and their inherited history, effects that I call *Inherited trauma.*

Given the large number of people affected by the Holocaust, survivor and generational trauma have been well studied and documented. Early researchers like Natan Kellerman realized that the field of psychiatry at the time could not adequately diagnose or treat Holocaust survivors: "The persistent anxiety, phobias and panic of survivors are not the same as ordinary psychosomatic disorders. Their depression is not the same as ordinary depression, and the degradation of their identity and relational life is not the same as ordinary personality disorder."[1] Kellerman found that traditional diagnosis and treatment in psychiatry are inadequate to the experience of Holocaust survivors and the generation following, because such diagnosis:

- does not fit;
- underestimates the unique nature of each Holocaust survivor;
- stigmatizes already disempowered people;
- blames the victims for their suffering;
- creates distance between the therapist and the patient;
  and,
- neglects the adaptive and successful coping abilities of the
  survivors and their families.

Kellerman believed that both Holocaust survivors and their children ". . . seem to suffer from inflexible and maladaptive patterns of perceiving, relating to, and thinking about the environment and about themselves. In the final analysis, there might be a need for a new category here also, such as *transmitted trauma syndrome*."[2] As I mentioned, I refer to transmitted trauma syndrome simply as *Inheritor Syndrome*.

I have attempted to compile and synthesize the traits (both negative and positive) of children of Holocaust survivors, as identified in a variety of studies, articles, and lectures. Like other children of Holocaust survivors, I have agreed with some of the findings and disagreed with others, and have generally thought that they do not quite get to the heart of our experience. I have commented on each trait, not for the purpose of definitively saying "yes, we are this" or "no, we are not this," but to offer additional pieces of exploration. You as the reader can come to your own conclusions. As you read these descriptions and my personal comments, you can decide what fits for you. In the first descriptor, for example, you might consider whether your traumatic inheritance has become a core part of your identity. What I don't want you to do is beat yourself up regarding any inherited flaws you might possess.

Traits of Children of Holocaust Survivors

1. The experience of the Holocaust is a core part of an Inheritor's identity.

Comment: Yes, it is definitely hard for us to create an identity apart from the Holocaust. The Inheritors I interviewed confirmed that, for them, the Holocaust is always a presence, even for those with happy childhoods. For example, many of us were named after the relatives who perished. It is customary in the Jewish tradition to name someone for the dead, never for a living family member, but after the Holocaust, this became especially meaningful. I was named after my father's mother, and my brother after my mother's father. Dina Wardi comments that we were given a role at birth to serve as *memorial candles* for a lost past and for those killed.[3] Sylvia, one of the dialogue participants, vehemently pronounced, "We were robbed of our identity!"

2. Children of survivors exhibit symptoms parallel to those associated with the concentration camp syndrome.

Comment: Dan Bar-On's observation goes beyond the trait just discussed regarding the Inheritors' strong connection with the Holocaust, and tells us that we actually exhibit traits as though we experienced the Holocaust directly.[4] This new awareness was an "a-ha" moment for me, something that I had never previously considered. The Second Generation Inheritors, unlike their parents, have *always* had the Holocaust in their life. Our beginnings started with the Holocaust. Miriam Greenspan, who like me was born in a Displaced Persons camp after the Holocaust, poetically captures this reality: "I felt I imbibed the Holocaust experience with my mother's milk."[5] Our parents, on the other hand, had normal childhoods and relatively normal parents. My mother's home life gave her strong roots and a rich cultural inheritance. She had pleasant recollections of regular picnics in the woods, or of belonging to various organizations with lots of cultural activities, singing, and lively conversations. I caught a glimpse of that culture in the documentary *The World Was Ours*. It was a thrill to see how vibrant her city was, but it also saddened me that we haven't had the benefit of knowing that rich culture. Instead, our childhoods were often about nightmarish stories and a sense of absence.

3. Inheritor Children absorbed the sense of death that enveloped their parents. Sometimes this identification with death became a central element of their personality.

Comment: Yes, the sense of death and danger of death was a given. My brother and I were not only afraid of death and thought about death often, we were also afraid of old people. Strange as this may seem, because we didn't have grandparents, nor did the other children in our community, we were not familiar with older people. "Old" people looked frightening to us. Perhaps it was simply because we lacked exposure to elderly people, or perhaps they represented death. I recall one evening when my parents were out, and an older person came to the door asking for money. We screamed in terror, slammed the door, and grabbed some kitchen knives that we kept by our side until our parents came home. We didn't tell our parents of the incident, not because we were ashamed of our behavior, since we felt justified about protecting ourselves, but because we couldn't share our fear with them.

4. The process of achieving independence from one's parents and the process of forming a separate and positive self-image is difficult for Inheritors. The psychological term for this is "separation-individuation" difficulties.

Comment: The inheriting generations carry a number of burdens. At the same time, the somewhat contradictory burden is that of separating their stories from their parents' stories. I can talk about separation-individuation by talking about our parents' perspective first. The traumatized parent clings compulsively to their children in the fear that their offspring may be killed or hurt. This is particularly understandable for parents who have held their children close to them as they hid in jungles and forests, or walked and traveled great distances to help protect them from certain death. It is not surprising, then, that in families of immigrants and survivors, *separation* often becomes associated with death. A child who does manage to separate (to leave home to go to school, to take a job, or to get married) may be seen as betraying or abandoning the family. Anyone who encourages a child to separate may be seen as a threat. Further, the survivor parents are emotionally unable to understand the child's needs, as the child is seen as an extension of them, and every failure or difficult event or emotion becomes catastrophic. "This intolerance of their children's autonomous growth and separation resulted in greater family enmeshment for the children after the Holocaust."[6]

The problem of *separation-individuation* is at the core of the child's inability to form a personal identity, which often appears undefined, unclear, perhaps not grounded or a little *spaced out.* This is at the core of the difficulty of Inheritors, or even the *gifted child* in Alice Miller's terms, to fully achieve autonomy. Many Inheritors do find strategies for overcoming these demands, and successfully create autonomous lives, perhaps experiencing a little guilt on the side.

5. Because of their parents' over-protectiveness and extreme anxiety, Inheritors may either develop a strong capacity for functioning and adaptation, or the opposite may occur, and they become fearful, afraid to take risks and unable to adapt to changing circumstances. Some are able to separate from their parents and live their own lives, while others prefer to be alone, and others never achieve separation.

Comment: Given our parents' extreme levels of insecurity, they wanted to provide maximal security for their children. Unfortunately, in their efforts to secure their children's safety, the message they relayed was that danger was imminent, and they enforced all kinds of restrictive demands. These parental fears added to the Inheritors' difficulties in separating. Many Inheritors can't swim and are not particularly good at sports, because our parents did not encourage us or allow us to venture out or take risks. This came up in our dialogues:

> **JUDITH:** My father was afraid to teach me to swim, but he carried me on his back as he swam. They wanted to be normal, but they couldn't be, and we were miracle children so they needed to protect us. I cannot judge it; it wasn't easy. I had to accept the burden. We didn't want to hurt our parents.

ESTHER: The overriding difference was the protection of my parents. They knew nothing about the culture in the US. For me, it was overwhelming protectiveness and fear. There was fear about everything. I was not even allowed to have a sleep-over with a friend. Because I am independent and a good kid, I had a great deal of difficulty with that control. Now as an adult I think it made me very much of a loner.

The dilemma about the extent to which we protect our children versus setting them free is one that all parents face. I reflected on this parenting dilemma in this poem.

I Wish I Were a "Yah-No" Mom

*As time goes by, I wonder about the emptiness
left behind by the "No"
I wonder about the sadness that grew and grew
with each "No."*

*How can I say "No" to the children I love,
When I can still feel the empty craters ground deep
inside
With each denial still resounding in my head.*

*Who will soothe them? Will they recover?
Will they be stronger, more resilient, and more resourceful?
Will they find their own way?*

*Do I have the courage to say,
"Yes" to their ability to do it themselves,
"Yes" to my ability to sit with myself.*

*I knew a woman who would answer questions with
a "yah-no"*

I never knew which answer she was giving,
but things moved ahead anyway.

I wish I had been a "yah-no" Mom
And my kids would never have empty craters to fill.
They would say: "Mommy, I can do it by myself,"
And, "Mom, you're not the boss of me,"
And, "Mother, I know what I'm doing."
I would simply reply, "yah-no,"

  Because in the middle of yes-no,
  There are no fearful unknown futures
  Theirs or mine

    There is only
    "I can choose"
    And if I get it wrong
    "I can choose again."

6. The psychic and emotional closing-off of Holocaust victims from other people served as a defense mechanism to hide from the past, compelling them to distance themselves from others, especially their relatives.

Comment: This observation about the compulsion to emotionally distance from relatives explains the inability of my mother and her siblings to maintain sustained connections. Their over-sensitivity would plunge them into arguments that would result in years of estrangement. Our family lost connection with the few family members who remained alive—two aunts, one uncle, and our only two cousins on my mother's side. There was no family on my father's side. That their need to protect themselves from strong emotions actually created fierce emotions during these estrangements seems paradoxical. As children who were exposed to these moods, and who absorbed and assimilated their messages, we, too, were required to find ways to close ourselves off from all the pain. We, too, needed to close off from the chaotic emotions.

To protect myself when I was younger, I put on a veneer of coldness and distance although it was not real; underneath I was unbearably sensitive. I also spoke in a low voice, so that I wouldn't say anything that would set off my mother. Another reason for my quiet voice was because I never wanted to sound harsh, loud, or downright scary as did my mother. In my adult years, I realized this voice didn't serve me, and I worked hard to express myself assertively and to speak with a fluid voice that would be heard and respected.

Children of Holocaust survivors and children of alcoholics face similar challenges. In the book *Adult Children of Alcoholics,* I found we shared one highly significant experience, the unpredictable behavior and roller coaster emotions of one or both of our parents.[7] In my case, I experienced this with my mother. I never knew who I would find on the other side of the door when I came home from school. I could have been met by a funny, charming mother or a screaming, hysterical, frightening and frightened person. My father was resigned to her moods and rages, explaining that she was nervous and that I should not argue with her. Now, of course, we would say she probably suffered from PTSD. Indeed, I was very moved by my mother's pain, but I didn't know how to soothe her or how to protect myself. I wrote this poem about my mother's pain and my empathy for that pain, as well as what I felt to be my responsibility for that pain. I now realize that I was not responsible for her pain, but at that time, I was helpless to understand this, nor could I possibly have known what I could do.

A Mute Appeal

Help the giver of my life
Help the taker of the death
and life I deal to her

Stop up her heart at the penalty of stagnation
Stop it up anyway

7. Narcissistic union with the parents makes Inheritors the rescuers of those who died, as well as the rescuers of their own damaged parents.

Comment: This is an accurate description of one of our burdens. We tuned in to our parents' every mood, and we had the responsibility of keeping them from descending into despair or becoming overly anxious. We also never shared our own problems, such as our difficulties adjusting to a new country. "To be a good daughter was to be a happy one. It doesn't seem as if it should be such a burden to have a mandate to be happy, but it is. We were to help our parents in their projection of assimilation."[8]

8. Survivor mothers are unable to clearly and directly provide their daughters with all the love and feeling they need; they are unable to tolerate the daughter's feelings of pain, anger, aggression, or her desire to compete or rebel against her mother.

Comment: This observation was certainly a reality for me, but I think many daughters everywhere have had this experience. Any expression of emotion on my part, especially sadness and heartbreak, was met by my mother with angry admonishments to not cry or with disparaging humor: "There goes Niagara Falls again" was her sarcastic joke about my easy tears. My mother loved me so much she couldn't bear for me to be in pain, given she herself was in such chaotic pain. At the time, of course, I didn't have this awareness.

9. The overprotective behavior and constant reminders from their parents of potential dangers led Inheritors to develop cynicism, phobias, lack of trust, and feelings of victimization.

Comment: In my younger years, my parents' overprotectiveness was suffocating. I wrote this angry poem, which, when viewed in this context, also shows me the lifelong self-doubt that surrounded me and the self-doubt that followed me.

My Mother Has Two Sisters

My mother has two sisters
Called Doubt and Disappointment
Their dark shadows hovering around me
At my every turn
Always nearby

Nattering in my mind.
"Be careful
Better watch out
You'll be disappointed
You'll cry

You don't know enough
You're not strong enough
You're not pretty enough
You're not smart enough
You'll cry, you'll cry."

As my mother and I grew older, my perspective changed, and instead of finding her protectiveness annoying, even suffocating, I found her protectiveness amusing and endearing, as exemplified in this story about her warnings of danger.

My mother at ninety-three suffered from dementia. Words didn't come to her easily. Following one visit, as I was preparing to leave, she said, "Wait. Don't go. I have something to say."

She struggled and struggled, but the words didn't come. So I asked, knowingly, "Do you want to say 'Be careful'?" Her excited response was, "Yes! Be careful, be careful! Don't go where you shouldn't!" Rather than feeling the anger those words used to generate, I left with a tear in my eye. Now that I understood more about the *Inheritor Syndrome*, I had compassion for what lay behind those fears.

Fortunately, I was able to take reasonable risks in my lifetime and to overcome the fears my parents tried, without avail, to instill in me. The irony is that the resilience, resourcefulness, and tenacity that I also inherited from my parents helped me to overcome my fears and distrust of others.

10. Inheritors are either hostile and mistrustful of gentiles, or they rebel and date or marry non-Jews.

Comment: To say dating non-Jews is a rebellious act is rather simplistic. I dated and married a non-Jewish man. I believed that, after the catastrophic event of the Holocaust, there would no longer *ever* be hatred, racism, and genocide again. I would serve as a torchbearer, rather than a "memorial candle," breaking with a narrow view of culture, as I saw it, to become a citizen of the world where religion and race would no longer be a force of divisiveness and exclusivity.

I also wanted desperately to fit in, to escape the isolation that came with being a kind of refugee, a child without an extended family. There was no one around to take some of the pressure off our small family unit. I thought I would marry into a "normal", extended family where people weren't so emotional and where I could feel more normal myself. I wanted to have the ability to harness all that emotionality without losing my soft heart. That my marriage did not deliver on my hopes is unfortunate.

11. Inheritors experience more guilt than the norm.

Comment: Dan Bar-On identifies a paradox. The combination of childhood preoccupation with, and guilt for, parental sadness, added to the belief that one is not entitled to personal happiness, sets the stage for pervasive and persistent feelings of guilt. The Inheritors suffer guilt simply because their circumstances are so much better, even though they realize that this was what their parents wanted for them and is due to their sacrifices. "Life is a matter of unrelenting seriousness."[9] This quote captures the combination of guilt, sense of responsibility, and drive for success that motivates many Inheritors and many immigrants in general as well.

12. Inheritor children tend to be more alienated and experience a greater degree of autonomy.

Comment: This is a strange combination of traits, and also seemingly contradicts the earlier description of our lack of autonomy (as related to our difficulty to separate from our parents).

In areas of personal decisions, even decisions about education, I did have a greater degree of autonomy than the norm, and I thought nothing of it. I accepted it as how life works. For example, when I began high school, I was in a class that was called the Practical Stream. Someone from the administration came into our room, and told us that if we planned to go to university, we should be in the Science Stream. I didn't know if university was in the cards for me, but I thought quickly and decided on my own that it would be best if I switched streams. I immediately changed classrooms without consulting with my parents.

Similarly, when it came to deciding on my area of study in university, I was in control of my decision. What I particularly loved about my autonomy was that my readings were never censored, and rules or religious teachings were not imposed on me. I formed my own opinions, and was appalled if anyone deigned to question this freedom. Since my parents couldn't help me with homework, I was never micro-managed and pressured by them. In that sense, I think they raised me in a post-modern parenting style, that of giving me the freedom to be a self-regulating child.

Regarding the trait of feeling alienated, a nagging sense of feeling different and set apart from others seems to be a familiar experience for almost all adolescents, not just Inheritors. What might have made it harder for us as Inheritors is that our parents could not help us with validating our feelings or with helping us to find coping strategies.

The feelings of alienation is certainly part of the immigrant experience. In one of our dialogues, Kathi honestly describes this feeling: "I was ashamed of being a newcomer. I would say I was from Canada. I didn't have my dates pick me up at home, because my parents spoke with an accent and I was ashamed of them. I wanted to fit in."

On reflection, I would prefer to think that experiencing alienation as well as autonomy can have both positive and negative consequences for all of us. It has given us a greater awareness of our own and a compassion for the difficult experiences of other people.

13. Loss in general, and the loss of important figures of the past, had an impact on our parents' affective resources (ability for emotional expression).

Comment: In our dialogues, the participants reported that the affective resources of parents varied widely. Some parents were warm, loving, and easy-going; others were harsh and demanding. Some were suffocating in their love, and others, distant and demanding. Further, the groups noticed that many variables could account for these differences. One variable was the age at which we emigrated. It seemed to us that the older we were when we left Europe, the more difficult the adjustment was. Another factor was the number of new countries that each of us went to. The more change, the greater the loss. The most impactful variable was the parents' survival experience. For example, it was important to know if they had been brave partisans who rescued themselves and others, or if they had run to safer countries in Europe and elsewhere, or if they had hidden with friendly families or hidden with abusive families. Were they jailed? Were they in labor camps or in the army? Had they been victimized and tortured in concentration camps?

One of the most important factors that emerged in the dialogues, and that I have observed in Inheritor families, is the personality of the Inheritor's parent and of the parents' parents *before* the catastrophic events interrupted their lives. What was their family life like? What kind of parenting did they receive? What were they like before the war? Depending on the answers to these experiences, one will likely observe different emotional responsiveness and capacities in the survivors.

My mother's friend Fela, who as a sixteen-year-old survived all the horrific trials possible in Auschwitz, nevertheless raised her five children with wonderful, positive energy and lots of laughter. I asked her once how she could behave like this when most survivors were so anguished. She replied, "My mother was that way." That was a new perspective for me. I didn't realize that people of that time could have had normal parents.

14. Inheritors suffer from depression due to over-identification with their parents.

Comment: I interviewed my cousin, Morris Shachter, with a view to determine if he suffered from depression, given his life-long devotion to his parents. His response reflects his strong identification with his father: "My father brings out the most emotion in me. I identify with my father when he says he lost everybody—the look on his face. I hate to see that in my father. My greatest anger is towards Germans for killing my father's six-year old sister, his eighty-year-old grandfather and his six brothers and sisters. I listened to his nightmares at night, and was sorry for my father for having to go through it. I just faced it, and dealt with it in a manner that let him feel better. It's important to do the right thing."

I believe that my cousin represents the majority of devoted children who identify strongly with the pain of their parents. I don't believe they are depressed, but rather that they are sad and angry over their parents' terrible losses. I would defend our right to our sadness or melancholy, perhaps a better term for depression. In the previous chapter, we also talked about the possibility that our so-called depression, both individual and collective, exists because we have not allowed ourselves to grieve.

15. Inheritor children become symbols of rebirth and restoration, creating magical expectations about undoing the destruction of the Holocaust and replacing lost families.

Comment: After trauma, people can usually find anchors and wisdom in their roots. But our roots were totally annihilated. Let me share a fantasy that I entertained as a young girl. I'm not sure that this is an example of a magical restoration of what my parents lost, but it certainly was a fantasy that would get me out of my family situation at the time. As a schoolgirl, I often lived in a fantasy world, sometimes losing all sense of time. One of my fantasies was that I had been mistakenly placed in this family, and that I really belonged to royalty. I would take the story plot to different places. In one story, I was a Princess who needed to have stones sewn into the bottom of her dresses so that they wouldn't fly up in the wind, which would be most unseemly. I didn't like the idea of being weighed down by stones, so I returned to my family with tears of guilt, imagining their grief at losing me. In all these fantasies, I always went back home. The chaos you know is safer than the chaos you don't know.

16. Survivors and their Inheritors are prone to excessive reactions to innocuous stimuli, authority figures, dogs, noise, etc.

Comment: Excessive reactions to real or perceived danger are known as *hyper vigilance.* It is a form of scanning the environment to determine what dangers might lie ahead. Hyper vigilance comes with the transmission of the trauma, and is also common in people suffering from Post-Traumatic Stress Disorder (PTSD). (I touched on this earlier in Chapter Two, under traits of Indigenous people/Native Americans, and again in Chapter Four, under Silent Memory.)

My parents were so afraid of authority that I would laugh as I watched my father check and recheck all of his pockets to see if he had his papers—*de papeerin*—whenever we left the country, though this was a rarity. He looked like a cartoon on a loop. My parents tried to instil their fear and anxiety in me in order to protect me. Much to their chagrin, this only led to risky and rebellious behavior on my part. At some level, I was counteracting my parents' often unreasonable fears so that I wouldn't get caught in that trap, that cage that was supposedly a place of safety.

17. Since most parents view luck as the reason for their good fortune to survive, Inheritor children view life as precarious and unreliable.

Comment: Though we may see the world as precarious—i.e., we cannot know what may be around the corner—what is also true for me and for virtually all of the Inheritors with whom I spoke is that we consider ourselves to be very lucky, and we expect that we will continue to be lucky despite the precariousness of the world. Certainly, we all consider our parents to be lucky, since it was ultimately luck that determined whether someone died or lived through the Holocaust. Every survivor has an amazing story of how luck played a part in surviving imminent death. Throughout this book there are stories of luck, such as that of my mother's closest friend, Fela Burman Wajcer, who survived Auschwitz.

Fela was in the line for the gas chamber along with her sister and her sister's young daughter. Fela's sister was beautiful, and a German soldier told her that she was in line to be gassed, but that if she would let her daughter go, he could save her and Fela. Fela's sister wouldn't leave her young daughter, but she did push Fela out of the line and commanded her to go to the other line. Poor Fela was never able to get over that day. She was sixteen at the time. From that day forward, she survived, as she told me when I was older: "I went through all of it, the marches, the diseases, the hunger, the labor, and always the selections." ("Selection" was a euphemism for being selected for death in the gas chambers, not the usual meaning of "selection" as a reward.) Another time she was selected for the gas chambers because she was covered with a body rash, which indicated that she had contracted a disease and could no longer be used as slave labor. Just in time, there was a commotion after Nazi guards found two girls who had hidden in a coal bin and were black from head to toe. Their appearance created such laughter and bedlam that it gave Fela an opportunity to switch lines. Fela and her son, Simon Wajcer, co-authored a book: *So You Can Tell: Prisoner 48378 Auschwitz*, in which she recounts in amazing detail her story of survival.[10]

In one of our dialogues, Bella told of how her father survived the gallows in Auschwitz. He was about to be hung, but the gallows collapsed during a bombing. This gave him an opportunity to run off and hide in the crematoria. He had a mark on his throat from the rope all his life. Bella's father narrowly missed death on another occasion because the number on his arm was smudged, and though his number had been called, he was able to claim that his number did not match it. I see this as a positive trait that has given us a high degree of resilience.

I would go so far as to propose that accepting the precariousness of life could also lead to resilience. Rather than allowing the vacillations of life to hold us back, change and the unpredictable may be viewed as challenges to overcome and opportunities to create new possibilities.

We will explore resilience further in Chapter Seven.

18. Among Inheritor families, parental praise and empathy is poor, while criticism is frequent.

Comment: I suspect that this trait is also similar to the experience of immigrant families, where parents' criticism is linked with high expectations of their children in the belief that their demands for excellence will protect children from economic hardship and ensure their survival. Nevertheless, in many Inheritor families, praise for the child is mostly communicated in conversations with acquaintances and friends. Most Inheritor children are well aware of their parents' pride, but they also feel the pressure of the high expectations.

To conclude this part of our conversation on the Inheritor Syndrome, it seems that these observations can be helpful if we accept what our reality represented: that our parents, who loved us fiercely, were generally poor at expressing their sadness, and that their emotions came out in different forms (worry, hyper-arousal, rage, emotional outbursts, fear of authority, etc.). It's possible they were afraid that, once they began to express their sadness, the dam of repressed emotions would burst, and they wouldn't be able to stop it.

In closing this section, I offer a poem that evokes the alienation and the burdens of an immigrant who represents any age, any culture, and any trauma. I wrote this as an evening student in university (I worked during the day) about one of my classmates, many of whom were immigrants and couldn't afford to attend classes during the day.

The Immigrant

Great country this Canada
I go to the University at night
Nice place
Pretty girls
I better not get in the way

Smiles

I'm very tired

Looks around

Maybe I'll buy a nice modern suit

Looks around again

This music these young people play
Not so bad
I'm happy here

Taps foot

Wish I could get rid of this headache

Rubs forehead

I feel a little lost
Wish my family could see me now

Frowns

They wouldn't understand
But they would be proud
Must have cost a lot of money this building

Grimaces

Wish I had had this when I was young

Taps foot nervously

Hard this course I'm taking
My kids will be luckier

If another war doesn't come.

Burdened Parents, Burdened Children

I tried desperately to erase the sadness we inherited.
It couldn't be erased. I, like the others, absorbed it.
I, like the others, took on the sadness as my own.
                                    —Elie Wiesel

I would like to delve deeper into some of these inheritor traits—in particular, the inherited burdens that come with our strong identification with our parents. Klee's illustration looks precisely like its title, *Burdened Children*. I interpret some of the boxes as representing the parents or perhaps history which envelops and *boxes in* some of the other boxes that represent the burdened children. The children look like they are struggling determinedly to move forward.

Survivor parents faced a difficult dilemma when they became our parents. They could not escape their painful memories; they were plagued with fears for their children, and yet they needed to build from scratch a life for their families. Their children also faced a difficult dilemma: empathetic to their parents' intense need for protection from their nightmares and their fears, they took on the parental role while still young. It was as though both the parents and the children lived in each other's skin. Carol Kidron describes an Inheritor who always prepared shoes at the foot of her bed in case she needed them in a hurry. It seemed that this practice connected with her mother, who had no shoes when she walked in the snow on the death marches.[11]

The following discussion during a group dialogue reflects the layers of this burden for Inheritor children:

YOSSI: There was a reversal of roles. We were the parents to our parents. It was always: what would we do without you? They were emotionally dependent on us. They lost opportunities for life because they were young when the war started, so they lived through us.

DOUBI: I felt my father was jealous—"How dare you enjoy life when my life was so miserable?" But I wouldn't pay the price for him.

ESTHER: Maybe that is your resilience.

DOUBI: It wouldn't help to complain. Whom would I complain to?

GITA (questioning the group): Did we have to adapt more than other people?

YOSSI: I had to compensate for my parents. We lived two lives, theirs and ours. We could not express our concerns or minor or major miseries and small failures, like less than perfect school grades. They didn't hide their misery and their misery took precedence.

DOUBI: My father was the center of attention; everything was based on his needs. The best thing was if we stopped breathing.

ESTHER: It is hard to differentiate if our experience is based on culture, educational background, or the Shoah.

DOUBI: Itzik and Yossi, do you, as psychologists, have tools to help you cope with this?

YOSSI: We found ourselves studying psychology, though we had other plans. Itzik was going to be in law and I was going to study biology. We needed help in understanding our fathers. Each night I heard my father scream and watched him run around the house like a mad man; he was trying to escape from the ghetto.

DOUBI: My son is the joy of my life; I adore what he has become. The moment he told me, "I know why you are the way you are: it gave me . . ."

ITZIK: Relief?

DOUBI: Yes. Relief.

The following is part of a story written by one of our dialogue participants, Judith Maier. She titled it *A History Lesson*. Similar to Itzik's and Yossi's experiences, Judith also regularly heard her parents scream at night, even though during the light of day they tried to shield her from their pain. This story captures not only the event of her mother's testimony at the trial of a Nazi commander, Dr. Sturm, but also Judith's identification with her mother, even to the extent of sharing her mother's breath. This is an excerpt of Judith's account.

At first the defense tried to undermine her credibility. She had to undergo all sorts of tests to prove that her memory, and her sanity were intact. They made great effort to shatter her self-confidence, barking questions at her, trying to confuse her; question after question almost on top of each other, not giving her a chance to answer. Abruptly my mother stood up, and facing the defense team spoke in fluent German: 'Just like the Nazis didn't succeed in exterminating me, so you won't succeed in confusing me! Everything is carved in my memory, the town, the ghetto, the camps, the horror! A Nazi murderer is the accused, not I.'

Pale and shocked, the judge stuffed a little white tablet into his mouth. Sternly he ordered the defense to stop their interrogation. The trial continued. 'Is there anyone familiar to you in this court-room?' one of the prosecutors asked my mother. Without hesitation, she pointed at the defendant and replied: 'I recognize this man as Dr. Sturm, Obersturmbannführer, the deputy commander of Lublin and area, who did not hesitate to stain his own hands with our blood.'

As if, at a command, all ten defense lawyers leaped from their seats, shouting, gesturing. 'Your honor! This witness must be called to order. Dr. Sturm never killed anyone. He only obeyed orders!'

The judge popped another tablet into his mouth and told the defense lawyer to sit down and not interrupt the witness testimony. He then turned to my mother and asked gently: 'Did you see the defendant kill anyone?'

I looked at my mother, my heart beating fast for us both. I prayed that she wouldn't break down. That she would, eventually, reveal everything that burned inside her for so many years! And she didn't let the opportunity to pass. She was much calmer, cooler than usual. Her voice was clear and firm although I could detect excitement. She gave details and accurate dates.

During one of the actions, that is before thousands of Jews were sent by wagon to their death, the defendant stood above the crowd on a platform, introducing himself as the new commander, in charge of law and order. 'Is there anyone present here, named Sturm?' he asked. From amongst the thousands crowded together, frightened, a white-bearded old man pushed his way forward. 'My name is Sturm,' he said. He was ordered to approach the platform. When he was close enough, Dr. Sturm took his pistol from its holster and shouting: 'Me Sturm, and a Jew Sturm? Only I am Sturm!' He shot the old man.

My mother related the last sentence in a low voice. It was quiet in the court-room. No one moved. The judge looked worn out. His hand searched for the pill-box. My mother said that she could also reveal other incidents. From time to time I felt her breath being extracted from her and I imagined my soul flying with it. In order to continue, she would sometimes sip from a glass of water. My mouth felt dry as I watched the movement of her lips. The judge on his platform became paler and paler—the pill-box became emptier and emptier.

When Judith looked at Klee's drawing, she found it reflected exactly how she felt, carrying the burden of her parents' pain, which she mirrored so realistically in her story above. She noted that the children are tiptoeing so as not to disturb or upset the parents. She also saw in the drawing her "struggle not to be sucked into a deep well." That is a good description of my struggle as well, though I manifested it differently. My coping strategy was a sort of angry rebellion.

However, Judith and many others wouldn't dream of showing anger at their survivor parents and add to their pain.

This is how Bella, also a dialogue participant, described the mask she had to put on for the sake of her mother: "My mother was in a labor camp, not a death camp. Today she is eighty-three and is really very strong for what she's gone through. She's always afraid, though, and very needy. She doesn't know about me (Bella was fighting cancer). I can't say she's been a wonderful mother. I was her life but it was a sick situation. You feel you have to be perfect. I was always smiling; no one knew how I felt. I had to do everything perfectly so I shouldn't upset my parents. That's difficult for a young girl to go through."

Inheritor children certainly have a tall order to fill. Yet we could not, and did not, walk away. It was our *cherished burden,* as I prefer to call it. Many accepted this burden without anger. I, on the other hand, experienced a boiling cauldron of something akin to indignant anger even as I submitted to my lonely role. I wrote this untitled poem about my frustration in carrying the burden of my parents' emotions.

> *Don't burden me with your cares,*
> *I bear them already.*
>
> *Don't burden me with your woes,*
> *I've wept over them already.*
>
> *Don't burden me with your fears,*
> *I've quaked over them already.*
>
> *Don't burden me with your needs,*
> *I've wanted them already.*

I first became aware that I was on my own at the rather early age of four. When I was that age, I threw rocks at my father, or so the story is told; I have a recollection that this action was quite deliberate. I know why I threw those rocks. I was angry that my father seemed so weak and wasn't taking care of me as he should. Elie Wiesel said, "We grew up orphaned while our parents were still alive, protecting our parents from their pain while there was nobody around to protect us."[12] Nevertheless, we carried our burdens like precious, precarious bundles into our adolescence and on into our adulthood. We didn't shed a tear in self-pity.

We did feel alone and lonely for a number of reasons. We lived in a kind of void, with only a notional idea of what life was like for our ancestors before those traumatic events. The destruction of my mother's town of Vilna, considered the cultural capital of Poland, signalled the virtual destruction of the Ashkenazi culture and language (European Jews, as opposed to Jews from the Middle East and other countries), leaving my generation with a deep sense of a lost past. Having no *before* is like living with an impenetrable mystery, a mystery that sits internally at an unconscious or repressed level and continues, for me, until the present. We had no grandparents to tell us about earlier times. Our parents didn't have the capacity to be present for us. We had few, if any, uncles, aunts, or cousins, and we felt like a minority, not only among our French-Canadian Catholic neighbors, who called us names and threatened to beat us up, but also in the Protestant culture and school system. We also felt like we were different among the Jews who were born in Canada; they were wealthier that we were, more self-assured, and they didn't have any idea that we had this Holocaust cloud surrounding us. We were *the greener,* the greenhorns, the immigrants.

Yes, the Holocaust trumped everything: our own feelings, our own struggles, our own needs. Nothing added up to much in comparison with the Holocaust. We had the job of sorting out our parents' stories. We had the job of sorting out why our families were killed. We had the job of understanding why people didn't speak up and defend their neighbors, and why so many became the complicit aggressors. We had the job of sorting out why the world allowed so many people to be killed. We had the job of sorting out frightening words like *Gestapo, gas chambers,* and *numbers on arms.* And we pondered the unanswerable: "Why were we so hated? What made us so different?"

At the core, our biggest challenge was separating our story from that of our parents. Mary Rothschild wrote, "I have learned that I cannot save my mother from Auschwitz and that giving up my life will not restore hers . . . Yet in the telling of my story, I learned to create meaning out of the ashes of my murdered relatives, my mother's traumatized life, and my own years lost to the task of healing. I learned to separate my story from that of my mother."[13]

In a sense, it would be fair to say that it wasn't my parents who had left me with a void, a sense of isolation; it was the Holocaust itself. I always felt as though the Holocaust happened to me. It happened to me because I had to carry the weight of our history. It happened to me because I had to take care of my fragile, fearful, emotional parents when I was still a child. As an adult, I still feel emptiness within emptiness as I try to fill it with people, knowing they are not responsible for my void. So instead, I fill them; I fix them; I rescue them. I let them off the hook because I am afraid of losing what I don't have in the first place. Like trying to find the right size of suitcase, I try to find the right fit of a house, the right career fit, the right man, someone or something that can fill the void of the child, Gita.

Most of us will agree that we were taught about surviving, not about living. Our imaginings were about putting ourselves in the shoes of the many people who perished, like Anne Frank. I would ask myself these questions as I sat in a classroom in elementary school: Would I have survived? Would I have given in if I was being tortured? Would I have turned in my parents to the Gestapo? What does it feel like to be hungry? Is there pain? How do you die from hunger? Does it hurt in the stomach? Could I bear to live in a concentration camp and see people dying all around me? What is it like to have your toes fall off from the cold? (One of my mother's friends lost her toes this way.)

And if that wasn't enough, I invariably judged myself as unworthy, unable to survive. "No," I thought. "No, not me; I couldn't do it." And I would feel guilty for my failings and cowardice. I didn't know about partisans, or I might have had more heroic imaginings. No child should sit at school and ask themselves such questions. Helen Epstein says, "The guilt leaves no room for joy."[14]

Without the capacity of our parents to support our emotions or even tolerate difficult or sad emotions, many of us were left feeling isolated and alone. This poem describes my sense of sadness and isolation.

Song of Gita

I am a bird woman
Circling the world
Seeking solace
From the sorrowful notes
That beat without measure
Reverberating from one heart to the next.

I sing to myself as I fly
I sing to myself as I cry
My own song of Gita
Known only by me
Understood alone by me.

At night, I tuck myself under my wing
And find comfort there
A pause from the endless, meaningless refrains.

The trauma of war, victimization, and racism affects people everywhere, even here in Canada. Thousands of Japanese Canadians were interned in camps in Canada, and their possessions were taken away in the wake of the December 1941 attack launched by Japan on Pearl Harbor. One of the child Inheritors of this event is one of our most famous and beloved Canadians, the world-renowned Canadian scientist, television personality, author, and environmental activist, Dr. David Suzuki.

In television interviews, Suzuki talked about his family's experience. He was five years old when his family was ordered to leave their home and their dry cleaning business, which was sold by the government under a new order-in-council, the Custodian of Enemy Alien Property.

Suzuki, his mother, and two sisters were interned in a camp from 1942 to 1945. His father had been sent to a labor camp in Solsqua two months earlier. Suzuki's sister Dawn was born in the internment camp. He has said that this experience made him realize the fragility of democracy.

Canadian Inheritors of parents and grandparents who served in WWII, who were captured as Prisoners of War (POW) and who worked in labor camps in Indonesia and Korea, or who have served in more recent wars such as Iraq or Afghanistan, are familiar with inherited pain. I met a Canadian veteran's grandson who bears a tattoo honoring his grandfather; he spoke of the tattoo with great emotion. Veterans will often say that they are not the same person they were before the war.

Many immigrants, who have come to Canada to make a new life, bear the scars of war, economic or environmental disasters, and separation from their families and culture. Many are thriving, but many struggle with PTSD and inherited trauma. I feel a strong empathy for immigrants, and the current plight of refugees brings me to my knees.

Burden of Guilt: Perpetrators, Collaborators, Bystanders, and Collective Guilt

This chapter would not be complete if we didn't talk about the burdens carried by another group of Inheritors: the Inheritors of the perpetrators, collaborators, and bystanders. There are also those who haven't self-identified in any of these ways, but whose descendants have a sense of collective, if not inherited, guilt. When I visited Europe, I could feel that collective sense of guilt over the crimes committed against Jewish citizens. It is generally not spoken about, but when it is, the pain is visible on people's faces. In the Netherlands, where I have travelled when speaking about the large numbers of their Jewish population who were sent to their deaths, their communications were almost wordless. "It should never have happened!" they would simply say to me. My readings, observations, and conversations bring me to the conclusion that the reckoning is still not complete, and I fear that German children of perpetrators who avoid confronting their history are doomed to suffer for many more generations.

I was encouraged upon reading a recent interview in *The Guardian* with Bernard Schlink, the German author of *The Reader* (also a successful film by the same name) in which Schlink addresses the lack of confrontation of German guilt. Schlink believes that German children today still have to deal with the difficult hand history has dealt them. He describes his own German identity as ". . . a huge burden, but it is an integral part of me and I wouldn't want to escape it. I have accepted it." Furthermore, he believes that many of his friends and colleagues have done much to disguise their "Germanness," to assume other identities in an effort to escape the sometimes-overwhelming historical responsibility. He believes that the burden of nationality has shaped the way in which Germans view themselves, their responsibilities within Europe, and their keen show of solidarity with the rest of Europe: "We Germans tend to prefer to see ourselves as world citizens . . . or Europeans rather than as Germans (whereas the underlying) desire is to escape the guilt attached to being German . . . This idea will always fail, because a German who goes to France, England, the United States and presents himself as European will find out the world is not as cosmopolitan and international as we'd like it to be."[15]

Mary Rothschild provides her personal account of such a confrontation when she participated in a dialogue between Inheritors of the Holocaust and of Nazi perpetrators. Rothschild's account, as with all Inheritor accounts, begins with her mother Ana's experience in Auschwitz and then her own Inherited experience. "For her, the war did not end with liberation . . . I am confronted with that reality ever time I look into my mother's eyes . . . [We] grew up with concentration camp nightmares, torn between a mother to whom my joy was too much stimulation and had to be squelched, and the rest of the world to whom the vast reservoir of pain was too discomforting."[16]

Since I am interested in the dialogue process, I was interested to read about Rothschild's experience of a dialogue between adult children of Nazis and Jewish Inheritors. Before she talked about the dialogue, she described her distrust of Germans because, among other things, they repeatedly claim that they didn't know what was happening. She notes the experience of Colonel Hayes, the liberator of Buchenwald, who, despite being familiar with the carnage of war, was unprepared for the horrors there. What haunts him to this day was the smell of the dead and dying. Yet Germans who lived in close vicinity to these camps claim they didn't smell or see anything. So when Rothschild entered into her first Jewish/German Dialogue in 1992, she was certainly apprehensive and sceptical.

Rothschild was relieved to hear that Jewish participants were there "not to forgive the unforgivable but to address it." There were two facilitators on the perpetrators' side and two facilitators on the survivors' side. One of the participants was a child of a non-Jewish Polish survivor of the concentration camp, a reminder that Hitler targeted not only Jews. The Jewish participants grappled with whom to hold accountable, since these descendants of their Nazi parents were innocent. The German participants talked about pushing against a collective conspiracy of silence to get to the unbearable truths. Moreover, they revealed that, in Germany, one must have permission from the spouse of the perpetrator to do research into a parent's Nazi past, describing "... a system designed to perpetuate the legacy of silence and the subsequent collective sickness . . ."[17]

Rothschild found her "emotional restitution," as she calls it, when one of the German facilitators said, "I am so sorry for what our parents did to your people." With each "I'm sorry" —which many spoke, for the first time, on behalf of the guilty who could not or would not say it—they made amends, and Rothschild's heart opened. They confronted the Holocaust together, not separately, and felt that they were set free from their burdens. She provides us with a wonderful quote by a German poet, Ursula Duba, that might be helpful to all who grapple with German guilt openly or secretly: "The challenge of Second Generation Germans is to not mistake the futility of the guilt with the necessary expression of sorrow."[18]

By the end of the dialogue, Rothschild describes their group as no longer German or Jewish, but rather ". . . a group of people sick with despair over what happened fifty years ago. Perhaps such dialogues, like an alchemical process, can transmute the guilt and anger through recognition and understanding into something meaningful and productive and prevent our legacies from being passed on like a defective gene to the next generation . . . There I actually experienced that the solution to stereotyping is to know each person one by one, to look into their eyes, to receive their story and to respect the sacredness of their being."[19]

My personal experience with German guilt happened when I was eighteen and attending university. An older professor, a married German handsome man, proposed that I have a child by him and that we would spend a year in Europe, after which I would give him the child. I understood by his explanation that he wanted a child specifically by a Polish Jewish woman. He had been sixteen in Germany during the Holocaust, a Brown Shirt who was being primed to become a Nazi soldier. He was old enough to know what was happening, but not old enough to object, he told me. In a way, he was in between being a perpetrator and being an innocent young man without power. At the time, I simply thought he felt guilty and his worst crime was that this request was egotistical and selfish. Of course, I didn't agree to take part in his plan.

After reading Simon Wiesenthal's book, *The Sunflower*, I realized the full meaning behind the professor's request, conscious or unconscious on his part. In *The Sunflower,* Simon Wiesenthal relates an experience he had in Auschwitz, when he was asked for forgiveness by a dying Nazi, a young man covered in bandages. This man had been brought up as a strict Catholic but was responsible for burning people alive, men, women and children; he locked them in a building and listened to their cries. Wiesenthal listened to him without responding each time he was summoned, never knowing if he would meet his own end with each visit. He would go back to the camp and have discussions on forgiveness with his friends in the camp. In the end, he walked away without a word.

The second half of Wiesenthal's book is a series of essays by world-renowned thinkers who answer his call to comment on whether he did the right thing or whether he should have forgiven the Nazi. Most of the writers' responses focused on the question of forgiveness. Some gave Christian or Judaic interpretations of the question. Some commented on whether he had the right to forgive on behalf of the victims, and others remarked that, for the Nazi, any Jew would do to assuage his guilt, and so the young Nazi soldier was perpetuating victimization yet again.[20]

After reading this last interpretation, I had a realization about my professor's real intentions. If I bore his child, I, a Jew, would be serving as the mode for forgiveness, and he would be relieved of his guilt. The German-born Professor saw me as just another Jew who could meet his needs, regardless of mine. It was a form of victimization. My saying "No" was unknowingly my act of dignity and defiance, my way of announcing my humanity to someone who was prepared to dehumanize me.

Lots of lessons may be learned from this story about the necessity not to avoid confronting and connecting with our inherited history, and this goes for connecting and understanding with the history of others. At the same time, we need to stay positive, open, and caring, or we will be doomed to unknowingly repeat the trauma. The perpetrators, collaborators, or bystanders (many who immediately moved into their Jewish neighbors' houses even as the owners were being taken away), and those in between will be plagued with guilt that may manifest as anger and resentment, or may take other forms, such as abuse. This will be passed on to future generations. On the other hand, those who choose to take responsibility and take action for reconciliation will lighten their burden and, at the same time, lighten the burden of their own Inheritors.

Constructing Your Story

Chapter 7: Questions: The Inheritor Syndrome

- What is true for you in these descriptions of the Inheritor Syndrome and the subsequent discussion?

- What does not fit?

- Are there any emotions that you now accept as being understandable rather than as indicating a psychological problem? How will this awareness help you?

- Do you have a different perspective of the burdens your parents carried?

- Do you have a different perspective of the burdens you carry?

- On a scale of 1-10, how strong was your pain when you started to read this book?

- Doubi described the relief that he felt. Are you starting to feel some relief as well? Where are you a scale from 1–10 now?

8

THE SURPRISING LEGACY

OF RESILIENCE

There is a crack, a crack in everything
That's how the light gets in.

—Leonard Cohen,
Anthem

Post-Traumatic Growth

In the 1960s, Victor Frankl reminded us that Holocaust survivors shared a sense of hope and an unshakeable commitment to the unconditional meaningfulness and value of life in any and all circumstances. Frankl had the unenviable position of seeing the possibility of the human spirit in a concentration camp, and still was able to suggest the possibility of a positive emergence in the aftermath of trauma.[1]

Several models of personal growth and positive coping capabilities were developed, and by the 1990s, the Post-Traumatic Growth (PTG) model was introduced by Tedeschi and Calhoun. PTG theoreticians have found that the story a person constructs about their traumatic events can transform the trauma into a triumph. As Victor Frankl says, "We must never forget that we may also find meaning in life even when confronted with a hopeless situation, when facing a fate that cannot be changed. For what then matters is to bear witness to the uniquely human potential at its best, which is to transform a personal tragedy into a triumph, to turn one's predicament into a human achievement. When we are no longer able to change a situation . . . we are challenged to change ourselves."[2]

The neuroscientist Rachel Yehuda has remarked, "Almost nobody says after a rape, or being almost blown apart on a battlefield, guess what? I'm totally fine now! I'm back! If they are resilient, and they don't feel broken anymore, they can acknowledge that, but it's still not *back*. Forward, maybe, or, different in a positive way, or, I've somehow taken this adversity and transformed myself into a better version of myself, which some people call post-traumatic growth."[3]

Berger and Weiss have taken the PTG model to the family level, proposing that the family unit as a whole may grow, as well as the individual. This is dependent on the families' resources and characteristics before the crisis, including their finances, education, coping strategies, spirituality, adaptability, shared power, ability to communicate clearly and directly, boundaries, strong leadership, individual members' autonomy, ability to tolerate differences, spontaneity, ability to express a full range of emotions, collaborative problem-solving, and an overall sense of optimism. They identified that the family's flexibility to respond to life's changes was a crucial variable in their ability to respond to a critical event. For example, when a family member is diagnosed with cancer, this becomes a family event, and the family's ability to change roles helps everyone to cope and find new strengths. The story a family tells itself must change, though constructing a new story is a painful process.[4]

Zieva Konvisser's research on modern terrorism and politically motivated violence explored the resilience of victims following a terror attack, and focussed on several questions. How do victims deal with the memories of the attack? How do those who are indirectly exposed cope? How do they maintain a balance between fear and calm that allows continued functioning? Her approach was to discover and acknowledge the phenomenon of *post-traumatic growth*. Konvisser interviewed forty-eight survivors and their families in Israel. She found that post-traumatic growth can co-exist with post-traumatic stress. This is how those interviewed said they moved forward.

One of the respondents simply said, "The moment you decide to leave it behind and continue in life, then it's not just a matter of how you feel, it's a matter of what you decide—to act and to dedicate and to feel and to do."[5] Another person spoke of choosing to take a positive attitude along with positive action to move forward even in the face of obstacles by bureaucracy, banks, and insurance companies. One respondent spoke of his daughters' work at a camp that provides a special space for children of violence to grieve.[6]

Konvisser found that a family's search for meaning often leads to creative expression through commemoration activities and memorials, or through life-affirming activities such as education, teaching art therapy, good deeds, and activism: "Through these acts of *tikkum olam,* repairing the world, they repair their own hearts and souls and those of future generations."[7]

Two Stories of Resilience

As I grew up, I was aware of the efforts of my brother and other Inheritor children to adjust to a new country, a new language, even a new culture. They were determined to fit in, to learn, and to make their parents proud. It was as though they were working within two tensions. On the one hand, these young people were trying to move into a new world where they could be free of their burdens; on the other hand, they had no way of knowing how to move into such a world and how they could possibly ever be free of those burdens. As they grew up, I observed that some were highly successful and some barely managed. And I wondered what is it that makes the difference.

Now I ask the same question but with a slight addition: where did those who were able to succeed personally and professionally find the resilience to get on with their lives after inheriting the Holocaust, while others didn't have the needed capacities to live autonomous lives free of the burdens of inherited trauma? Because I have a strong sense that the answers are usually on the other side of the question, reframed as possibilities rather than problems, I thought I would take a look at my survivor parents. To that end, I would like to relate two precious stories of resilience, those of my mother and my father. Though the stories are about survival in extreme circumstances, some of the key traits of resilience that emerge from these narratives can be a clue to resilient traits that we as their Inheritors have the possibility of acquiring, and indeed many have done so. Just to be clear, when speaking of resilience in relation to Holocaust survivors and to Inheritors, it is not meant to paint the Holocaust in a positive light; it is intended to show those who have felt the obliteration of their past and of their identity that it is possible to find a way to get on with their lives.

IF I CAN'T GO THROUGH THE DOOR, I'LL GO THROUGH THE WINDOW

> *Every survivor has lived through a mythic trial, an epic odyssey.*
> —Eva Hoffman, *After Such Knowledge*

This is what I could capture of my mother's story, presented in her voice. Given that memory is not linear, the listener sometimes finds the stories to be incoherent and frustratingly difficult to follow. You may need to suspend judgement and to simply be aware of this reality, so that when you interview people, you will be able to allow their story to flow without trying to make it a logical progression. It was my son who interviewed my mother and it was amusing to watch him try to keep her to a linear, chronological account. I also noted, given my mother's strong ego, that she told the story from the frame of how smart she was and how people liked her.

LEA'S (LAIKA'S) STORY

"Vilna was a place where everyone always had something to do. Everyone belonged to one organization or another; everyone was involved in many creative activities. I was in the theatre and the choir. One day, before the *umglich*/catastrophe, I was in the woods with my friends and had a desire to simply lie down and sleep. I dreamt my Bubi/grandmother came to me carrying a basket of food. She told me: 'Shayna's (my mother's mother) children will be alright.' As it turned out, the dream came true—Shayna's children, my mother and most of her brothers and sisters, did survive. I was active in the Communist Party (she always whispered when she said this as if someone might overhear her and put her in prison, but not without pride in her voice). My father didn't like that I belonged to the Communist Party, but I was old enough to make my own choices.

The Communist Party told us that when it looked like the Germans were coming, they would help us. My best friend Frumele and I went to an empty factory according to their instructions. We were wearing our Communist hat and pin. We waited and waited but no one came. We could hear the bombs. I felt an urgency to get going and I told Frumele, 'I'm going.' 'Where are you going?' she replied with fear. 'Wherever my eyes take me; just away from here,' I told her. Frumele said she was going to go back home, back to her parents.

I ran to the train station. It was bedlam. People were everywhere. There was nothing such as buying a train ticket. I started climbing through the window and someone yelled, 'Laika, what do you think you're doing?' I answered, 'If I can't go through the door, I'll go through the window.'

On the train, a woman offered that I stay close by her and she would look after me. I was young and cute with bangs on my forehead. At one point the train stopped, because we were being bombed. We all ran out into the field and lay flat on our stomachs. When I got up, the woman was gone, but my brother was beside me. We went back on the train together. At one of the train stops, I overheard someone say they had an auto, a truck. I asked if I could go with them and help out with their baby. They agreed, and my brother and I continued for many weeks until we got to Middle Asia (at that time Middle Asia consisted of Uzbekistan, Turkmenistan, Tajikistan and Kyrgyzstan, as defined by the Soviet Union).

The Russians loved my singing and would call to me, 'Laika sing,' and I sang. I knew hunger; so did the Russians, but we had a place to stay, a room with seven people, and we were even given jobs by the Uzbeks. I worked in a sweater factory. Other girls stole sweaters for bartering, but I was an honest girl and I didn't steal even if that meant hunger."

My mother never saw Frumele or her own parents again. She survived the Holocaust in Tashkent, the capital of Uzbekistan. She credits the Russians for her survival. She continued to sing, sometimes with great patriotic or romantic fervor and sometimes with touching pathos, a learned ploy for survival when she felt threatened or when she felt insecure and needed to be accepted and cared for.

And my mother did survive. She also helped her brothers and sisters, whom she found in various twists and turns of events. I believe that her sisters and brothers must have arranged to get the necessary documents to them, as they tended to end up in the same place. Miraculously, of three brothers and four sisters, only one brother and one sister perished. The brother died in East Russia, as did her father; her sister, Henke, was shot when the janitor turned her in as a Communist. It was my mother who was the Communist, but her sister paid the price. Her mother, Shayna, hid in the attic and was discovered when she became hysterical and shouted out in fear. The Nazi soldiers shot her through the ceiling. How she came to have this information I do not know. Still, we can say her grandmother's dream came true, considering the impossible odds of surviving the Vilna ghetto.

My mother continued to be a force of nature, fiercely protecting my brother and me at the least provocation, often to my embarrassment. Today, her indomitable spirit informs everything I do. After many years of experiencing the contradictions and riches of her character—she was over-protective, fiercely loving, fearful, worried, sometimes hysterical, sometimes charmingly funny, scary, articulate even in English, uncannily intuitive, passionate, domineering, controlling, adorable, a lover of music, an actress and singer—I am now in awe of her. I give her credit for her positive influence on me. The comical picture of my short, twenty-four-year-old mother climbing through a train window has served me well.

My mother's particular tragic loss was that she did not become the person she could have been, given her talents and determination. My darling mother died at the age of ninety-three. I was with her the evening of her passing, or as I prefer to say, her expiration. Her last words to me were protective: "*Az ich bin krank, ees gei avek*/Since I am sick, go away." She let me know she meant what she said, and I reluctantly left.

My mother's story keeps me going forward whenever someone tells me that I can't do something; it is then that my resolve becomes still stronger. Her story signals some important characteristics of resilience: she had *chutzpah*—she was audacious, bold and non-compliant, intuitive, action-oriented, resourceful, and charming. She was a talented singer and could make people laugh. Both of these characteristics helped her to make friends. And of course, she had an ability to maintain presence of mind and to be watchful for opportunities that might prove fortuitous. I hope that I inherited some of these traits.

THE COMBINATEUR

> *I had two families.*
> —Zalman "Sam" Arian

My father's story is remarkable for its lack of detail. If only I had realized earlier how little I knew, I might have asked more questions. Now I encourage fellow Inheritors to ask lots of questions of all their older family members.

SAM'S STORY

My sweet, sad father would often talk about how he *combineered* to survive. It is a wonderful word which I knew to mean to combine this with that in order to get something else. Someone who is good at *combineering* can be called a *combinateur*. To be able to combineer is an important skill that can have a life or death consequence. For example, in Uzbekistan, where my father somehow ended up and where he met my mother, he worked in a bakery and stole bread for my mother and for her sister's family by putting the hot bread in his socks. That was combineering. It didn't matter that he burned his legs and needed to ease the pain by immersing his legs in warm water every night; he could trade that bread for food, shoes, coal or other necessities of life.

He was reported to the authorities for stealing, and was arrested. In jail, he contracted malaria, but my mother bribed the judge to get him out. Then, she contracted malaria, and it was my father's turn to help her. They helped each other, as did all war couples, which was how many of them survived. It is a wonder to me that survivor couples that did not marry for love but for their mutual survival managed a lifetime together. The repercussions on the Inheritors of these unusual liaisons are not well understood; or rather, Inheritor children are well acquainted with this reality, though it is not documented in the research.

My father, Zalman or Zygmunt, and then "Sam," was born and raised in Poland. He was movie star handsome. Sam was educated in both German and in Polish, given the complex historical connections of Poland with Austria. He married a lovely woman, Hela, his pre-war wife, as I think of her. She was from a religious home, but my father was not. Hela's father asked the rabbi if he should allow his daughter to marry this man who didn't even wear a skullcap. The rabbi asked Hela's father, "Is he good-looking?" Hela's father replied, "Very handsome." The rabbi answered, "Then let her marry him."

I have a picture of my father and Hela taken in Kraków in 1938. The couple appear well dressed and free of cares. No doubt, their two children, Henush and Helena, made them very proud. It is hard to believe that a few short years later, perhaps four years, this handsome couple would face humiliation and terror, and that my father's elegant wife and beautiful children would be dead.

My father explained to me that people were told that Jewish men were being sent to labor camps, and so his wife urged him to flee. When he learned that the lives of women and children were in jeopardy, he tried to get back, but was arrested. The story gets murky here. He was shot in the foot, but I don't know why or how.

I have much more to learn about my father. When he pronounced that he would never go back to Poland because he would be arrested immediately, I thought he was being cowardly. I now understand that this might mean he was considered to be an enemy of the state. Though I know he was arrested when he tried to get back to his wife and children, there is much I don't know. Was he in a Polish or a Russian prison? On what charge? How did he get out? Was he sent to Uzbekistan because he was considered a communist, a dissident, or an enemy of the state, or was he in Uzbekistan serving with an army? Which army? Polish or Russian? I take myself to task for not asking, but then, as Inheritor children, we couldn't, we shouldn't, and we didn't.

I have a possible explanation about how my father got to Uzbekistan, thanks to a fellow Inheritor researcher who painstakingly put together information about the Polish and Russian armies in the hopes of learning about her own father, who served in a number of armies. She informed me that the Russians, who used the Polish army, asked the men if they wanted to sign up for service or to go home. Those who said they wanted to go home were considered disloyal and sent instead to east Russia. That might have been my father's fate, which would explain how he ended up in Uzbekistan. It also explains why he said that if he ever went to Poland he would be arrested immediately. This also provides me with a clue as to why my parents' civil marriage happened in the town of Gorczakowo (English: Gorchakovo) in Uzbekistan, where a unit of the Polish army was stationed.

When my father said, "I had two families", I couldn't respond; it was too painful for both of us.

I wrote this poem about my gentle father in my late teens.

Daddy's Home

It's six o'clock!
Time for Daddy to come home

There's a fumbling at the lock
That's him, that's him!

A cold glow surrounds
The man who has brought
Karnartzel and cakes and chewing gum.

He blushingly watches our joyful acceptance
Of his offerings of love
Before even taking his coat off.

I am certain that my father's survival can be attributed to these traits of resilience: self-sacrifice, leadership, courage, and an ability to *combineer*—that is, to be versatile and resourceful as new circumstances arose. Both my parents had *Chutzpah,* a wonderful Jewish word that means bold, audacious, sassy, wily, shrewd, and clever, with a twist of rebelliousness and even rudeness.

My parents' stories mark the beginning of my compulsive journey to learn about my lost family and what my parents went through. My first stop was the Holocaust museum in Jerusalem. As a visitor walks into this magnificent piece of architectural design, set on top of a cliff with a beautiful view of the surrounding hills, he/she learns about the chronology of events as Germany invaded Europe. I was shocked to find that Vilna, my mother's city, was the first event of the Holocaust. My heart pounded as I wondered what I would discover! What I heard was indeed shocking and heart stopping. Vilna was where the horror began, in Operation Barbarossa in June 1941. My mother would have been twenty-three years old. Of one million Jews who lived in Vilna and its surroundings, only some eight thousand were fortunate enough to survive. The Jews who lived in the Lithuanian provinces were annihilated during the first few months of the war. These massacres included the obliteration of entire communities and the inhuman, unimaginable, face-to-face murder of utterly helpless people, including the old, women, children, and infants. Massive participation by the Lithuanians in the persecution and murder affected the dynamics of the Final Solution.

I understood for the first time that my mother was among the very few who survived. I was horrified when I learned of the Ponary massacre of one hundred thousand people, mostly from Vilna, about the time of my mother's flight. The executions took place between July 1941 and August 1944, near the railway station of Ponary. I asked myself, "Was this the same train station where my mother ran to escape? Probably!" My mother never spoke of this. She never mentioned Ponary. When we asked her if she ever went back to Vilna after the war, she replied in a matter-of-fact manner, "What for? There is nobody there."

How did my mother know to run when she did? She would not likely have survived if she hadn't made this spilt-second decision. Her attitude and action, reflected in her words, "If I can't go through the door, I'll go through the window," demonstrate the resourcefulness and sheer intuition that she drew upon to survive her many trials.

The opposite of *chutzpah*, is naïve. To be called naïve is a worse insult than to be called stupid. This is probably because, at the time the Nazi régime began, Jews did not believe they were targets for slaughter. Many identified themselves first as Germans, French, Hungarian, etc., and only secondarily as Jews. This naïveté was their death sentence.

In Israel, "chutzpah" has been given as one of the reasons for the stunning success of their innovativeness and entrepreneurship: "An outsider would see chutzpah everywhere in Israel."[9]

I would suggest "chutzpah" is a survivor trait of the different people who fled to Israel: Ashkenazi Jews (survivors from Europe); Mizrahi Jews (who were either expelled from Arab countries or chose to leave); Sephardic Jews (who came from Spain, Portugal), Ethiopian Jews; Arab citizens; and refugees, many from Eritrea, creating a unique, new culture.

A New Lens on Resilience

The *Oxford English Dictionary* defines resilience as "The activity of rebounding or springing back." It further defines resiliency as "elasticity; the power of resuming the original shape . . . the ability to return to the original position."

Much of the literature on resilience generally depicts models that support a definition of bouncing back from a traumatic event. For me, the idea of bouncing back like a ball does not fit. It is too light a step, too mechanical, given the burdens that we carry. I much prefer a construction such as this, by John Sigal: "Resilience is not a global personality quality. Persons may manifest resilience in some areas of their functioning and not in others. Everybody is right—those who report dysfunction in survivors and their families and those who report the opposite. In many instances, the discrepancies are due to the observers and the populations they observe."[10] As with all concepts, there is no single way to look at resilience in relation to traumatic events, given the variety of cultural, familial, religious, political, or economic contexts in which they occur.

Voices such as those of Victor Frankl and Elie Wiesel remind us that survivors have shared a sense of hope and an unshakeable commitment to the unconditional meaning and value of life in any and all circumstances. In fact, Elie Wiesel speculates about the reason neither the survivors nor the Second Generation became criminals, nihilists, or anarchists. "How is it that the members of a generation which has been brought up under the shadow of the holocaust and its losses and by traumatized parents, are able not only to get on with their lives, but to be successful and helpful and compassionate with their fellow human beings? . . . Quite the opposite . . . For to go through such upheavals . . . should have produced a generation of mentally unbalanced people (and their children too). It didn't . . .They began to build . . . reintegrated. . . . They became leaders. To me that is the miracle."[11]

Inheritors seem to have a variety of sources for their resilience. In the dialogues that I held with Inheritors, I routinely asked, "How did you move on?" The usual reply was that, though they carry much sadness, they are all right, and they even feel rather fortunate. Given their parents' stories of how luck played a role in survival, the transmission of a sense that "I am lucky" is understandable.

Zuhair Kanj, a young man with whom I have become acquainted, talks about the role of luck and quick thinking when he describes his escape from Syria to Turkey. He is happy to have me share this small part of his story.

Until 2010, Zuhair's life was normal: French school in Aleppo, then American School, then university studies in banking. He even worked at the retail shop, United Colors of Benetton. When the terror began, it was sudden, almost overnight. He had never seen anything like it. Heavy weapons appeared in the streets. Shell bombs started to fall, one hitting his family's house. They moved out and then back in again. On the fifth day of Ramadan, he saw fighting on the street. They fled to their aunt's house, but there it was worse: air strikes, the rebel army fighting the Syrian army. They went back to their house. They were stuck in the middle of the fighting. In Aleppo, he found himself out in the open in a rebel location when two snipers started shooting at him. He ran, not knowing which way to go, when an old man came running up and pulled him to safety. The old man's son was shot on the same street, in the same way, a week earlier. Zuhair declared, "I am a lucky man!"

Zuhair's instincts told him to take the bus and leave. The roads were still open. He picked just the right time before the borders were closed. He didn't tell his parents he was leaving, for fear they would talk him out of it. He cried the whole way on the bus to Turkey.

I would say Zuhair's resilience is demonstrated in his determination to survive, his independent spirit, resourcefulness, flexibility, quick thinking, and willingness to work hard. Having met him, I can also say his friendly, open, and curious manner is also a trait of resilience that assures him many friends and helpers. When I asked him what advice he has about living, his reply was, "It's hard work, but later, you will get rest."

Inheritors have also vicariously learned resilience from the role models provided by their survivor parents. Many of their parents, despite their trauma, did get on with their lives. They played cards with their friends, created various organizations linked to their individual communities from their countries of origin, engaged in energetic political debates, and earned a living. My parents and their friends were hilariously funny. They loved to dress up and show off their jewels and finery. Most of all, they delighted to see their loved ones well-fed.

That our search for information does not yield results does not matter. What matters is that we have taken the responsibility to surface the information about our lost past and our murdered relatives. My search regarding my siblings may be headed for failure, but I feel that love has motivated my efforts and I have passed their memory on to my children. A bookmark sold at Yad Vashem is inscribed with these words: "I should like someone to remember that there once lived a per-

son named David Berger." David Berger in his last letter, Vilna, 1941."
To David Berger and my siblings, there may be nothing more that I can
say than "We are remembering."

I am convinced that, along with all of the other factors that contribute to resilience, humor plays an important role. My son, a great
humorist and satirist himself, provided me with this quote, attributed
to Sid Caesar, about the meaning of humor: "Freud said that humor
is a way of dealing with our fears. I always believed that great comedy
derives from tragedy and from humanity. There's a fine line between
laughter and tears. When you laugh too hard, you start to cry. When you
cry too hard, you start to laugh. When someone doesn't know whether
to laugh or cry, your comedy is working." Jewish humor, as this quote
indicates, carries with it an acceptance of life's tragedies with an overlay
of ironies and paradoxes. While Jews account for less than 2.5 percent
of the population in the US, approximately 70 percent of the country's
working comedians are Jewish. Humor has served as a way of survival,
not only in life and death situations, but also in family situations. In a
recent CBC radio interview with Jules Feiffer, the cartoonist and satirist
was asked about what messages he received as a child. He responded, "I
had two messages. The first was that I had to succeed. The second was
that I was inadequate to do that."

My family's humor would certainly not be understood in "normal"
society. There was much welcome laughter, especially about the absurd
events and coincidences of life. For example, when each had thought
the other had perished, my uncle and his first wife were reunited after
people discovered they were both alive. Their respective spouses had
died. Everyone thought that, given their shared past, the couple might
end up romantically together at last. But they didn't like each other, and
went their separate ways. We found this to be a hilarious story.

Another theory of Jewish humor is that it served as a kind of
pre-emptive strike before an attack.[13] Much humor is characterized
by *semantic ambiguity*, the moment when one can see more than one
interpretation of the words. For example, Groucho Marx's classic jokes
depend on a grammatical ambiguity for their humor: "Last night I

shot an elephant in my pyjamas. How he got in my pyjamas, I'll never know." It is a device that sometimes intentionally causes confusion, and might provide another way of surviving by throwing a potential attacker off track.

With wit and humor, Woody Allen's tragicomic films explore questions of life and death, the existence of God, sex, guilt, crime, and the complexities of relationships, and they changed the movie industry. His film *Deconstructing Harry* ends with the erudite, complex, and yet funny line: "Rifkin led a fragmented disjointed existence. He had long ago realized all people know the same truth. Our lives consist of how we choose to distort it."

Leonard Cohen, a songwriter, singer, poet, novelist, philosopher, and humorist, has helped me in times of despair to laugh through my tears. I opened this chapter with the ironic quote from his powerful song, "Anthem": "There is a crack, a crack in everything; that's how the light gets in." "Anthem" tells us that, yes, people, countries, leaders, organizations, objects, and ourselves are broken, not perfect, but there is always a crack that lets in the light and helps us to move forward. The crack can always be reconstructed, like our collective, inherited trauma.

Franklin H. Littell, a Christian theologian, wondered what we are doing to reconstruct our messages. His own reply was, "We need the message of the survivors, of those who built a second life, to help us affirm life . . . We need to remember those who affirmed life, and to honor the survivors who built a second life, because we live in a life-denying century."[14]

The affirmation of life is a universal trait of resilience, to be sure! It tops the list of resilient traits I have put together to close this chapter.

Traits of Resilience

This list of the characteristics of resilience is built from the stories, dialogues, and concepts we have explored, as well as from the discussions about African Americans and First Nations inheritors. Taken together, a very strong list of resilient traits emerges. We have inherited and created these traits, and we can be proud of them. They certainly describe a process of surviving and moving forward from trauma that is far different than "bouncing back."

A resilient person may:

- Affirm life/a mission, have a purpose to live;
- Demonstrate *"chutzpah"*—a stance of being audacious, bold, wily, non-compliant;
- Show intuitiveness and an orientation to act;
- Charm, sing and laugh, and make friends;
- Maintain presence of mind, being present to fortuitous opportunities;
- "Combineer"—be resourceful in finding new ways to live;
- Demonstrate self-sacrificing leadership;
- Demonstrate non-conformity, risk-taking; desire for autonomy and freedom;
- Question, show curiosity;
- Devote self to parents; be generous with children and with friends;
- Refuse to be defined by trauma;
- Show tenacity; have a kind of stubborn, not-giving-up attitude;
- Use creative expression; be honest and generous in sharing information;
- Reframe the negative into the positive, see the glass half-full;
- Embrace the sadness, cherish the burdens;
- Feel lucky;
- Feel loved;
- Maintain humor, see the absurdity in life, live with ambiguity and paradox;
- Assume the role of holding the memory;

- Refuse to bow to outside pressure to revise or to repress experience;
- Feel indignation, moral outrage, defiance;
- Own a sense of the power of the individual in a hostile or rejecting world;
- Find joyful moments even in darkness;
- Take responsibility; take action;
- Tell their story/write their story;
- Decide to move forward;
- Discover their culture and history;
- Survive trauma, hardship, or loss;
- Love family and community;
- Adapt and cope successfully despite challenging or threatening situations;
- Have pride of community;
- Have intelligence;
- Intuit the environment and the emotional state of others;
- Show resourcefulness, be hard working;
- Build self-worth—for self and others;
- Determine to get an education;
- Determine to achieve personal goals.

Another Klee drawing, *"Angelus Novus" (New Angel but known as Angel of History),* may be illustrative of the survivor state. To adapt Walter Benjamin's interpretation of the *Angel of History,* the Angel (survivor) is transfixed by remembrances of the past, while at the same time he is trying to move away from the same past that he is contemplating. This tension between being in the past and also moving forward towards the future leaves the survivor stuck, paralyzed. His frail feet and small wings do not seem strong enough to push forward through the storm of the past.[15]

Angelus Novus/New Angel, Paul Klee, 1930

We can also look at the *Angel of History* as an Inheritor who is trying to fly forward while, like the survivor, he carries the weight of his inherited traumatic history. We might say that the angel (Inheritor) would like to awaken the dead, and make whole what has been smashed, but the storm of his inherited past has got caught in his wings with such violence the angel can barely fly. Eventually, the very storm propels him into the future, his back is turned away from the past and the pile of wreckage before him moves upwards to the sky. He succeeds to affirm life and fly forward.

A New Definition of Resilience

Putting the traits of *resilience* and the concepts of *social construction* and *post-traumatic growth* together, I would propose a new definition of resilience:

> *Resilience is the process of creating meaning out of the contradictions of life's darkness and light.*
>
> *It builds on the strength of relationships and community.*
>
> *It is the affirmation of life and of our own power.*
>
> *It comes from our experiences, observations, reflections, learnings, and what we have chosen to strive for.*
>
> *Much of our resilience is inherited from our parents and ancestors and is part of our collective humanity.*
>
> *It leads to growth, compassion and positivity. It provides us with life-giving forces.*

Constructing Your Story

Chapter 8: Questions:
The Surprising Legacy of Resilience

- What are your parents' survival stories? How do you feel about these stories?

- What traits of resilience did your mother have?

- What traits of resilience have you inherited from your mother?

- What traits did you once consider negatively, and now, having learned the back-story, can you reframe and understand them as positive traits to be proud of? Give some examples of times these traits helped you.

- What traits of resilience did your father have?

- What traits of resilience have you inherited from your father?

- What traits did you once consider negatively, and now, having learned the back-story, can you reframe and understand them as positive traits to be proud of? Give some examples of times these traits helped you.

- Which resilient traits do you possess that will help you to move forward?

- How does the definition of resilience resonate for you?

9

BIOLOGICALLY INHERITED HISTORY

*Being born into absence thrusts us into a space
where the past crashes at us from behind.*

—Ann Parry

A quick look at traditional methods to identify and treat traumatic stress, as well as a summary of long-standing and new research in biology and neuroscience might provide us with further insights into how survivors and Inheritors of trauma can move forward. Studies on generational trauma are not new, but what is new is the evidence that the transmission is not only psychological but also biological.

When I first started to ask questions about body memory, I was met with blank stares. I encountered even stronger negative reactions when I spoke about the memory I hold in my back. "Ah, that is in the realm of the paranormal," I was told. Today, the connection between mind, emotion, and body has been established.

The Stress Syndrome

Let us start with Hans Selye, whose theories on stress are familiar to most of us. Since 1936, when Selye published his theory of the General Adaptive Syndrome (G.A.S.), also known as the Stress Syndrome, the word "stress" has become part of our daily vocabulary. He identified the stages of stress as beginning with an alarm reaction, followed by the body's preparation for flight or fight. We know that too much stress is harmful to our health, but many of us do not know that Selye also found that a certain amount of stress can be an energizer and can promote our well-being and health. He called this positive stress, *eustress,* and negative stress, *distress.* When stress reaches our limit of adaptability, it becomes *hyperstress,* or (as we commonly call it, *burnout,* and burnout is toxic to our health. Importantly, Selye found the basis of stress symptoms was in the mechanism between the hypothalamus in the brain, the pituitary gland, and the adrenal system. My favorite quote of his is this truism: "Stress is an unavoidable consequence of life."[1]

Epigenetics

Epigenetics is an important new field of biology that has gained a lot of interest and is appearing regularly in scientific journals and the media. The part of epigenetics that is of particular interest to us is that it seeks to identify the mechanisms by which traumatic stress may permanently alter the molecules, neurons, cells, and genes of survivors in ways that are passed on to their descendants. This means that a surprising number of children of survivors may be less able to metabolize stress. While environmental/nurture factors are still key to the healthy growth of the individual, this science is seen as leading to a possible understanding of repeated racial, ethnic, and other types of violence.

Rachel Yehuda, Director of the Mental Health Patient Care Clinic at the Peters Medical Center and a professor of psychiatry and neuroscience at the Icahn School of Medicine at Mount Sinai Hospital, Ohio, is one of the world's leading experts in post-traumatic stress. Her research began by observing that Vietnam veterans had similar traumatic symptoms as the Holocaust survivors she had studied in her neighborhood in Cleveland, Ohio. A new study by Yehuda looked at the hormonal levels of cortisol in descendants of Holocaust survivors. Previously, it was found that many Holocaust survivors have low levels of cortisol and low levels of an enzyme that breaks down cortisol. However, unlike their parents, descendants have higher-than-normal levels of the cortisol-busting enzyme, while still having higher levels of cortisol. This suggests that the offspring of Holocaust survivors are less vulnerable to hunger but more vulnerable to the effects of stress, and they are more likely to experience symptoms of PTSD. These descendants may also be at risk for age-related metabolic syndromes, including obesity, hypertension, and insulin resistance, particularly if they live in an environment of plenty.[2]

The Academy of Pediatrics (AAP) reports that "the way genes work in our bodies determines neuroendocrine (nervous and hormonal systems working together) structure and is strongly influenced by experience. Trauma experience by earlier generations can influence the structure of our genes, making them more likely to switch on negative responses to stress and trauma . . . Never before in the history of medicine have we had better insight into the factors that determine the health of an individual from infancy to adulthood, a way of looking at life not as disconnected stages but as integrated across time."[3]

In the same report, LeManuel Bitsoi, a Navajo conducting research in genetics at Harvard University, is reported as saying, "Epigenetics is beginning to uncover scientific proof that intergenerational trauma is real. Historical trauma, therefore, can be seen as a contributing cause in the development of illnesses such as PTSD, depression and type 2 diabetes."

Another interesting scientific finding came to me from a conversation I had with my daughter-in-law, Hillary Baack. She seems to have acquired a strong emotional connection to my family's traumatic history, though her background is far from ours. When I asked her about why she thinks this is so, her explanation came from something she read that indicated she could have inherited the trauma of the Holocaust during her pregnancy with my grandson-to-be, since the baby's cells mingle with their mother's cells and pass on family genes to the mother. It seems that this is called *foetal-maternal microchimerism*, wherein cells are transferred between mother and foetus, knitting together our bodies, bones and brains as well as liver, lungs, thyroid and other organs. This cellular invasion means that mothers carry unique genetic material from their children's bodies, creating what biologists call a *microchimera*, named after the legendary beast made of different animals. A study of women who had died found that over half of them had male DNA in their brains, presumably from when their sons were in the womb. Foetal cells from fathers, their mothers and even grandmothers circulate through the mother's blood. We may harbor cells from an older brother, who may have given some cells to your mother, who then gave them to you.[4]

This would mean, then, that for me, my closeness to my siblings came through my father's DNA to me. Another way to look at my strong connection with my siblings!

Treatments, New and Traditional

While LeManuel Bitsoi finds epigenetics research on generational trauma interesting, he also notes that the Indigenous community's reaction to this discovery is: "What took science so long to catch up with traditional Native knowledge?" For many years, traditional methods have been used to help people surmount trauma and stress.

While the sciences are making inroads in understanding transmission of trauma, there are longstanding practices, such as energy healing, that have also proven effective for centuries using auras, chakras, acupuncture points and many others. I once went to a workshop where I was invited to hold my arm out and to keep it up as best I could while the other person pushed down on it while also, very rapidly, talking through a timeline of my life. It seems my arm weakened at three time periods in my life, the first being when my mother was in her last trimester of pregnancy with me. Though I did not pay too much attention to it at that time, my greater awareness of my mother's experience in the DP camp leads me to now believe that indeed, that might have well been my first trauma.

We are beginning to hear experienced psychiatrists propose that talk therapy does not work as well as other therapies for people who have suffered from traumatic events, children who have experienced repetitive sexual trauma, or people with PTSD. Meditation is recommended, as well as EMDR, which stands for Eye Movement Desensitization and Reprocessing. The American Psychiatric Association and the Department of Defence have approved EMDR. It is a form of *bilateral stimulation* in the mid-brain, where trauma is lodged, to enable a physical shift of the distress from the mid-brain.

Why meditation is helpful for people is explained by Daniel Goleman: "The big advantage of mindfulness practice is that it gives the brain a moment or two, hopefully, where we can change our relationship to our experience, not be caught in it and swept away by impulse, but rather to see that there's an opportunity here to make a different, better choice."[5]

I believe that talk therapy does work for many mental illnesses; however, group support can be equally or more helpful where validation and support by others who share a common experience is needed. This type of supportive intervention in a group setting, led by a qualified expert in treating PTSD, is demonstrated in the CBC documentary mentioned earlier, *War in the Mind*. In the documentary, we see the importance of role-plays by those who understand, and we see the emotional but burden-freeing breakthroughs that can happen. I am sure that the veteran legions are important to war veterans because it is such a place, a place where they can gather and speak with others who have had similar experiences.

Epiphanies can happen in conversations with groups of people like us, and also with people who are from another cultural experience. Conversations in peer support groups, with initial training for the group on how to self-manage, are springing up in the U.S., where health costs are so high. Talking openly and honestly with family and friends can be helpful as long as the language used is not negative, but rather with the intention of a positive exploration to finding a way of being together or to help with finding a new way in dealing with a problem. It is why I used dialogues rather than interviews to run my research with Inheritors, knowing that more discoveries that might have remained in the unknown would be generated in a dialogical space and that transformations might occur. Indeed there were some breakthroughs and transformative experiences, as you have seen. (Chapter Eleven speaks some more about dialogues as a process for validation and transformation.)

The Arts for Overcoming Inherited Trauma

We've talked quite a bit about the value of creative arts, for accessing memory and unknown knowledge as well as for appeasing the pain in our souls. Lora Beldon, an artist who grew up as a "military brat", describes an interesting example of how art can be used as tool to calm the brain. She understands well what the effects of a parent with PTSD can do to a child Inheritor's small brain since she grew up in an environment with a father who is a Vietnam vet and suffers from PTSD. Her first insight came to her when she was eighteen years old and she drew what her brain felt like. The drawing looked like a tornado spiralling downwards. She immediately understood that her problems retrieving information from the past were probably because her brain was stuck in hyper mode, much like trying to catch a car swept up in a tornado. This experience led her to learning about neuroscience, early childhood development, military brat culture and PTSD among Veterans, Holocaust survivors and their inheritors. In 2008 Lora started a Military Kid Art Project, aimed at helping military brats from ages five to eighteen across the U.S. More recently she has begun working with adults, particularly veterans and their families.

I found one of the exercises Lora Beldon uses particularly interesting, as it seems to generate an increased feeling of well being similar to the feeling of well being following from an EMDR treatment. Lora's students are invited to incorporate a repetitive pattern within their design that helps support their story.

For example, if a child drew imagery of a ship leaving port with a character waving goodbye, they might choose to create a very stylized wave pattern that has controlled repetitive circular lines. She has found that students can concentrate for long periods of time on repetitive lines. This helps to empty the mind while also creating a new neurological response to a stressor; a more healthy response is created and this shift out of the brain becomes a body memory. In other words, the trauma is moved out of the intractable repetitive trauma patterns in the mid-brain.

We can say that art is any activity that puts one *in the flow,* where one forgets the stresses of life and enters into a place of play and fun. That isn't to say you need to be an artist. Aside from theatre, music, dance, photography, etc., an inventive spirit, openness to new ideas, shifting the way you do things, taking an appreciative—even humorous—view of the wonder of life and nature, will help you unleash from burdens, past and present, and calm your mind, body and soul. Just watch a child 'in the flow" and you will know how to be in a place of presence and play.

Constructing Your Story

Chapter 9 Questions: Biologically Inherited History

- How do you think you might be affected by PTSD or by biologically inherited trauma?

- What do you think will help you to find relief from emotional suffering?

- What would being in the world without the burdens of trauma look like? You can answer this question any way you want. Whatever comes up is the right answer.

10

THE UNIVERSAL QUESTIONS

Historians are futurists because history repeats itself.

—Alexander Baack,
Third Generation Inheritor, Filmmaker

Three Universal Questions

Two of the profound burdens that Inheritors carry are the need to confront their past, as we are doing together through this book, and to confront the eternal questions about evil and forgiveness in light of the cruelty that was perpetrated on our families and ancestors. This chapter is not intended to provide any definitive answers. You know by now that I don't do black and white, or this is right and that is wrong. We live within paradoxes, moving back and forth between the yin and the yang, and are often faced with irresolvable dilemmas. What we can do is talk about these questions, explore the writings of wise men and women, and most importantly, sit with these questions even if we can't answer them, so as not to get stuck in the questions and give up hope. Just the sitting with the questions is good enough. It is one of the ways that will help us to move forward.

The three key universal questions are:

1. Was this evil an anomaly (just happened once to one person or a people) or is evil innate in human nature?

2. How could so many regular people in so many countries sit by or even help with the killings of their fellow human beings?

3. Is forgiveness possible?

Knowing your history and the history of others is important not only because they give us clues to the possible answers to these questions, but also to serve as warning signs of danger ahead. We have talked about World War II and how the Nazis and their allies killed over twelve million people and displaced countless others. The Japanese killed over ten million Chinese. Countless millions of Black Africans were murdered or died in slavery, and countless millions of Aboriginal peoples in many countries from Turtle Island (North America) to New Zealand, Australia, and South America were treated as non-beings and killed without remorse.

Zygmunt Bauman, a sociologist originally from Poland, has this to say about how these horrors and killings could have taken place, especially in Germany, the heart of one of the most civilized parts of the world. He believes it should be seen as deeply connected to modernity: its mechanical, order-making efforts, its procedural rationality, the division of labor into smaller and smaller tasks, the taxonomic categorisation of different species, and the tendency to view rule-following as morally good. It is modernity, he believes, that played the primary role in making the Holocaust come to pass. He also argued that, for this reason, modern societies have not fully taken on the lessons of the Holocaust; it is generally viewed—to use Bauman's metaphor—"like a picture hanging on a wall, offering few lessons."[1] According to Bauman, it is an important lesson to learn, given that this is the way our society currently operates, within a mentality of rational problem-solving aimed at reaching a set goal.

The filmmaker Claude Lanzmann took another approach to helping us understand the depth of evil that man is capable of. Lanzmann spent eleven years creating the documentary *Shoah* about the Holocaust, conducting his own interviews and refusing to use a single frame of archival footage. Dividing Holocaust witnesses into three categories—survivors, bystanders and perpetrators—Lanzmann presents testimonies from concentration camp survivors, an Auschwitz escapee, and witnesses of the Warsaw Ghetto Uprising, as well as a chilling report of gas chambers from an SS officer at Treblinka. *Shoah* is considered by many to be the defining film in the history of dialogue between Holocaust memory and the question of how it should be portrayed on film. Still, despite so much effort, the question remains: how can we explain the cruel behavior? As Simone de Beauvoir, author and existentialist philosopher, says about Lanzmann's documentary: "After the war we read masses of accounts of the ghettos and the extermination camps, and we were devastated. But when, today, we see Claude Lanzmann's extraordinary film, we realize we have understood nothing. In spite of everything we knew, the ghastly experience remained remote from us."[2] Nevertheless, as we will see in the next chapter, what the documentary did succeed to do was to provide historical validation.

An interesting study to help us find a possible explanation for how ordinary people became mass murderers was postulated by Christopher Browning, an American historian and a contributor to Yad Vashem's official, twenty-four-volume history of the Holocaust. He was compelled to look into this when he noted that, in mid-March 1942, ". . . some 75 to 80 percent of all victims of the Holocaust were still alive, while 20 to 25 percent had perished. A mere eleven months later, in mid-February 1943, the percentages were exactly the reverse. At the core was a short, intense wave of mass murder. The centre of gravity of this mass murder was Poland."[3]

Browning found extensive collections of indictments for virtually every German trial of Nazi crimes conducted by the Federal Republic of Germany's office for coordinating the investigation of Nazi crimes. There he found the indictments concerning Reserve Police Battalion 101, a unit of the German Order Police. Unlike other testimonies he had read, he found this one "had a feel of candor and frankness conspicuously absent from the exculpatory, alibi-laden, and mendacious testimony so often encountered in such court records."[4] Browning's analysis provides a unique insight into how the Nazi régime was able to coerce ordinary, middle-aged police officers into becoming murderers.

What he discovered helps answer the question: "How could this kind of evil have happened?"

What Browning found was a multiplicity of factors that influenced Reserve Police Battalion 101, including the combination of the effects of war, constant racism, propaganda and indoctrination, peer pressure, desire for praise, prestige, and advancement, loyalty to the group, propaganda of German superiority and incitement of contempt and hatred for the Jewish enemy. He is known for saying: "Nothing helped the Nazis to wage a race war so much as the war itself. . . . it was all too easy to subsume the Jews into the image of the enemy."[5]

At the end of his book *Ordinary Men*, Browning takes us from the war into contemporary times, and offers an observation about modern society similar to that of Zygmunt Bauman:

> "The collective behavior of Reserve Police Battalion 101 has deeply disturbing implications. There are many societies afflicted by traditions of racism and caught in the siege of mentality of war or threat of war. Everywhere society conditions people to respect and defer to authority, and indeed could scarcely function otherwise. Everywhere people seek career advancement. In every modern society, the complexity of life and the resulting bureaucratization and specialization attenuate the sense of personal responsibility of those implementing official policy. Within virtually every social collective, the peer group exerts tremendous pressures on behavior and sets moral norms. If the men of Reserve Police Battalion 101 could become killers under such circumstances, what group of men cannot?"[6]

What an ominous answer to the question!

Universal Implications

We are living in cruel times. Our television screens reveal thousands of vulnerable children taken by their families into dangerous situations to escape even more dangerous situations. They board treacherous ships to cross over turbulent seas or walk across many miles of hostile lands to end up in precarious situations or refugee camps. They witness death and experience betrayal, hunger, cold, the indifference of strangers, and so on. The world has been stricken by the sight of refugees drowning and starving, with over sixty thousand people displaced from their home countries. There are families who have been severed and relocated throughout the globe under various conflicts and disasters. The counsel we have heard by Alice Miller, Mary Rothschild, and Aboriginal oral wisdom has told us that we will perpetuate the burden of trauma and guilt to the next generation and the generation after. This has critical implications when we consider the millions of suffering families around the world today. We can expect that these children will, of necessity, sublimate their needs for the sake of their parents and their family's survival; these children, as much as their parents, will need much emotional and psychological help.

The Foreign Press reported that children of Syrian refugees in Lebanon have lost hope and are committing suicide. A twelve year old girl, who was treated after taking rat poison, was asked by her mother why she tried to kill herself. She replied, "Mama, there are seven of us and you work and work to feed us, but you can't keep up. Without me, there will be one less person to feed."[7]

The Inheritor experience is readily identifiable everywhere if we were open to seeing it. The first step, however, is to recognize it. In 2010, when thirty-three Chilean miners were rescued, the media, politicians, and miners were front and center. Watching the news, I noticed a child of one of the miners. He was standing to the side, clearly stricken, afraid, and confused. Yet, all the attention was on getting video of his father who was the first of the rescued miners, as he emerged from the mine. Indeed, one of the reporters practically pushed the child aside. I worried about that child, thinking, "There it is! Second-hand Inherited trauma!" I still wonder if that child ever got the support he needed at least from his parents.

The children in Klee's drawing are not identifiable as belonging to any race or religion. They are children who have inherited difficult legacies. We, like Klee's children, are universal beings, and we can and will make a difference.

Constructing Your Story

Chapter 10: Questions: The Universal Questions

1. Was this evil an anomaly or is evil innate in human nature?

2. How could so many regular people in so many countries collaborate and help with the killings of their fellow human beings?

3. Is forgiveness possible?

11

MOVING FORWARD

*Every moment each human being is doing the best
we know at that moment to meet our needs. We
never do anything that is not in the service of a need;
there's no conflict on our planet at the level of needs.
We all have the same needs. The problem is in the
strategies for meeting our needs.*

—Marshall B. Rosenberg,
Founder of Non-Violent Communications

Historical and Political Validation

All of a sudden, the people who had survived became legitimate.
— Judith Maier, Dialogue participant, referring to
the Eichmann trial

As we have seen, there was no opportunity for Holocaust survivors to make sense of their conflicting experiences and feelings; neither were there opportunities for their children, the Inheritors, to make sense of their inherited burdens or even their own identity. The silence was finally broken in 1961 with the Eichmann Trial, and with it came validation, but not without a lot of controversy. Deborah Lipstadt noted that: "In the United States, the story was the lead item. CBS said the news had electrified the world as though Hitler himself had been found."[1] Some condemned the kidnapping of Eichmann from Argentina, while others argued that the trial constituted retroactive justice. According to Lipstadt, the basic realities were that there was no international body to try Eichmann; Germany did not actually want to try him there. She quotes the German newspaper, *Frankfurter Allgemeine*: " It is not to us to question the Israelis as to where and how of the arrest . . . It is of no importance where Eichmann is brought to justice."[2] The debate continued, and the logistics were complex: who would judge, prosecute and defend Eichmann? Israel had to prove that Eichmann would receive a fair trial.

The debate came into my life as well, but for me personally, it provided a positive side effect—indeed, a life-changing moment. I was in my pre-teens, attending a meeting in a room with two large tables seating twenty-five people per table. At my table, I was the only one arguing that the trial should be in Israel. I had always been shy, and I never spoke in public. I was shaking inside, but I was stubborn and did not give in to the older and more authoritative voices. I was embarrassed when we reported a vote of twenty-four to one, with me representing the lone number one. The embarrassment turned to pride and happy surprise when the second table reported twenty-four to one in the reverse order. Had I sat at the other table, I would not have had to fight for my position, but I also would not have had the occasion to find my voice and learn that "I know what I know." This important sense of *knowing* is often lost once girls reach their adolescence, according to Mary Field Belenky.[3] In this case, I never lost my sense of knowing; it faltered, it diminished, but I held my ground, probably marking the beginnings of my own form of resilience.

Eichmann's trial in Israel left an important legacy. At last the victims were no longer vilified for "going to their deaths like sheep to the slaughter," an unfortunate interpretation of the words by Abba Kovner when he rallied the remaining people in the Vilna ghetto to fight as partisans in the woods. "The trial of Adolf Eichmann served as therapy for the nation, starting a process of identification with the tragedy of the victims and survivors, a process that continues to this day."[4] Today it is recognized that Holocaust victims were caught up in a machine that could not be resisted, and are seen as heroes and martyrs. Even resistance in the form of simple acts of kindness, like sharing a morsel of bread, is seen as an heroic act. This is a form of validation; it is an affirmation of life and the dignity of man.

Historical validation can come as commemoration as in the establishment of memorials and museums, where the realities of the past are recognized and those that were victimized are honored. I have described a few of the new museums of African American history and have discussed the impact of museums commemorating the Holocaust on their visitors. At the National Museum of the American Indian, an important exhibition opened in 2014. "Nation to Nation: Treaties Between the

United States and American Indian Nations" reveals an important and unknown part of American Native history that has been deliberately kept secret. An excerpt from the exhibit website is presented below.

"For the first time in history, one of the eighteen treaties negotiated and signed during the Gold Rush between the United States and the American Indian Nations of California, but secretly un-ratified by the United States Senate in 1852, went on display. The Treaty of Temecula, also known as Treaty K, was just one of the eighteen treaties that was submitted to the U.S. Senate on June 1, 1852 by President Millard Fillmore. Unbeknownst to the Native nations' signatories, the Senate rejected the treaties and ordered them to be held in secrecy for over 50 years. Left undefended by United States Armed Forces, Native nations across California were overrun by white settlers and American Indians subjected to violence at the hands of state and local militias. Considered illegal aliens on their own land without state or federal legal recourse, it led to their ethnic cleansing. The American Indian population in California plunged from perhaps 150,000 to 30,000 between 1846 and 1870. The 1880 census records 16,277 American Indians in California—a 90 percent decline in their population since the onset of the Gold Rush. A letter by California Indian Affairs superintendent Edward F. Beale to U.S. Commissioner of Indian Affairs Luke Lea, Chairman Grubbe: 'The wretched remnant which escapes starvation on the one hand, and the relentless whites on the other, only do so to rot and die of a loathsome disease, the penalty of Indian association with frontier civilization . . . I have seen it, and seeing all this, I cannot help them. I know they starve; I know they perish by hundreds; I know that they are fading away with startling rapidity; but I cannot help them . . . They are not dangerous . . . It is a crying sin that our government, so wealthy and so powerful, should shut its eyes to the miserable fate of these rightful owners of the soil.' Seeing this treaty on display is both horrific as it shines daylight on the cheat and fraud that accompanied the sale of our land . . . [But] this is validation."[5]

Validation in the form of a formal apology is critical in easing the anguish of past injustices and violence. Here are excerpts from an open letter of October 8, 2015 to David Cameron, President of Britain from the former Prime Minister of Jamaica, P.J. Patterson, telling him that Jamaica deserves an apology from Britain for slavery:

> The 180 years of slavery in Jamaica remain fresh in living memory . . . [The] 180 years were followed by another 100 years of imposed racial apartheid in which these families were racially oppressed by British armies and colonial machinery. The scars of this oppression are still alive in the minds and hearts of a million Jamaicans . . . To reject this living experience is to repudiate the very meaning and existence of these people's lives. How can we simply forget it and move on to the future? If there is no explicit admission of guilt now, when will be the proper time? Contrary to your view, the Caribbean people will never emerge completely from the "long, dark shadow" of slavery until there is a full confession of guilt by those who committed this evil atrocity . . . We invite Britain to engage in removing this blot on human civilisation so that together we can create a new and secure future.[6]

Everyday Validation

What we have seen in these historical and political accounts is the need by a people for validation of their suffering. The validation comes from the felt knowledge that their suffering has been seen, has been witnessed. Validation occurs daily: birthdays, remembrance days, family memoirs, YouTube, Facebook, nights out with friends; all of these large and small channels help provide the witnessing of a person's very existence. When I was studying education in teacher's college, I recall reading that one of the worst things a child could say to another is "forget you." One of our deepest fears is to be erased, discounted, dismissed! That is the case at the individual, family and nation-to-nation levels. We are a whole system and all of these interconnect. The witness is anyone: parent, friend, boss, political leaders, etc. who fully hear someone's story with compassion.

When Roger Ebert, the great film maven, published a review of Lanzmann's *Shoah* in 1985, he captured the concept of "witness." The important act of witnessing the experiences and feelings of an "other" is key to helping Inheritors of trauma to move forward. This is a small part of Ebert's review. Many parts of the review are too graphic to repeat here but are available on his website, RogerEbert.com.[7]

> "For more than nine hours I sat and watched a film named *Shoah*, and when it was over, I sat for a while longer and simply stared into space, trying to understand my emotions. I had seen a memory of the most debased chapter in human history. But I had also seen a film that affirmed life so passionately that I did not know where to turn with my confused feelings. There is no proper response to this film. It is an enormous fact, a 550-minute howl of pain and anger in the face of genocide. It is one of the noblest films ever made."

After a graphic testimony of the inside of the gas chamber by a man called Muller who was responsible for leading people inside and then doing the terrible task afterwards, Ebert reflects:

> "Always before, in reading about them [the gas chambers] or hearing about them, my point of view was outside, looking in. Muller put me inside. That is what this whole movie does,

and it is probably the most important thing it does. It changes our point of view about the Holocaust. After nine hours of *Shoah*, the Holocaust is no longer a subject, a chapter of history, a phenomenon. It is an environment. It is around us . . . It is not a documentary, not journalism, not propaganda, not political. It is an act of witness. In it, Claude Lanzmann celebrates the priceless gift that sets man apart from animals and makes us human, and gives us hope: the ability for one generation to tell the next what it has learned."[8]

Eckhart Tolle, widely recognized as one of the most original and inspiring spiritual teachers of our time, talks about *pain body* which he describes as a kind of energetic entity that takes possession of the human body and is used to generate more pain. Tolle believes that Jewish, Black and Native Americans (Aboriginal people) have a *collective racial pain body*. Tolle says the pain body "has its own primitive intelligence, not unlike a cunning animal, and its intelligence is directed primarily at survival . . . In most people, the pain body has a dormant and an active stage. When it is dormant, you easily forget that you carry a heavy dark cloud or a dormant volcano inside you."[9]

Tolle suggests that, in situations where a child has strong pain body manifested in screaming pandemonium, the parents must reflect on their own pain body; parents need to give voice to their own awareness if they want to help the child become aware and give voice to their emotions. He provides advice that, at the heart, is about validating the child's emotions. He suggests that the parent might ask questions that would help the child become aware of hidden feelings so that they can be released, thus helping him or her to cope better with those feelings whenever they arise. Parents might ask, "What image came to you when you were upset?" "How did you feel when you were upset?" "What helped you to feel less upset/scared?"[10]

Given what I believe about trans-generational pain, if a parent wants to give their child the space to be in touch with their emotions and thereby manage them, it makes sense that the parent should be aware of their own pain as a first step, and then to act as a validation instrument and as a witness in order to be truly helpful to the child. It would be necessary, then, for the parent to have had the benefit of telling their story to someone who can listen with compassion. This is how Janusz Korczak puts it in his book, *Loving Every Child: Wisdom for Parents*, which is considered the first book written on the rights of children:

> "Know yourself before you attempt to get to know children. Become aware of what you are capable of before you attempt to outline the rights and responsibilities of children. First and foremost you must realize that you, too, are a child, whom you must first get to know, bring up, and educate."[11]

Validation Through Conversations and Dialogues

In sacred space an individual can suffer what he always needed to, and lacked the courage.
—Carl G. Jung, *"The Undiscovered Self"*

Another way we experience validation on a daily basis is in conversations with close friends and family. There is much we can learn from one another. Liza, a lovely person who lives in the Netherlands and is not Jewish, on hearing my story realized that she too had an Inheritor trauma much like mine. She hadn't connected the fact that her parents' experience (they were interred in a Korean concentration camp but had never talked about it) had something to do with her own search for understanding her depression. The story of Liza has a happy ending. She and her sisters asked their parents about their past; they had an honest and open conversation, and the validation and repair began quickly for the whole family. There were two conversations at play here: the first one between me and Liza, and the second between Liza, her sisters, and her parents.

My numerous years working at all levels as a consultant to orga-nizations and, more recently, as a facilitator of dialogues for communi-ties who have experienced trauma, have convinced me that most needs can best be served through the process of group dialogues. What do I mean by dialogues? Conversations are an everyday, life-long real-ity for all of us. These include our inner conversations with ourselves that happen on a constant basis. A dialogue stretches conversation to a place where transformation and new understanding is possible, if it is based on active listening and sharing of ideas, feelings, and needs to take place in a safe space. It is important for the Facilitator to take a *not-knowing* stance in order to be truly present to the individuals in the group. Harlene Anderson describes dialogical conversation as "a conversation in which people are talking *with* each other and not *to* each other . . . [it] is a mutual search for a shared understanding. This does not mean full agreement. It is always developing and in this development, new meaning emerges."[12]

When I facilitate a group dialogue, I check in with myself to make sure that I am in touch with my inner dialogue so that I don't influence the outer dialogue with my own emotional needs or biases. You may have already noticed that I am an equal participant in the dialogues that I have described. I put on my facilitator hat only when necessary; most of the time I am an active and interested participant. I take this role in all my dialogues for a number of reasons. I want the space that I create to indeed be sacred and to model that we honor the voice of everyone in the circle equally. I do not want to create a you-versus-me scenario or a scenario in which I would be viewed as the "authority," especially given Inheritors' acquired sensitivities to authority figures. I also want to help people to feel that they have agency and power, particularly if those feelings need some nurturing.

I have found that group dialogues serve the need for acknowledg-ment and validation of inherited trauma. When I speak of validation, I refer to validation by another person, a witness who acknowledges our experiences. The "other" can be anyone who is willing to enter a con-versation and be compassionate to the anger, the hurt, and all the feelings in between. To this end, I have gathered Inheritors in small groups, hoping that, by sharing their narratives with others, there would be a new awareness that could transform the trans-generational progression of the trauma.

My first dialogues were with Inheritors of the Holocaust. Since then, I have begun to work with communities of Inheritors from various parts of the world. The dialogues have brought together people whose individual experiences varied. Some people inherited legacies of death and victimization, and suffered as a result of their parents' trauma; others led idyllic childhoods despite their parents' trauma, while others inherited heroic legacies of a parent or parents who had performed heroic acts. One person inherited the trauma of 9/11; another, the tragic death of a loved one; another, a family member's difficult cancer journey.

I usually find that magic happens when people are in conversation. What surprised me with the dialogues with Inheritors was the lively energy in the room, the sense of a special event, of people coming together to talk about themselves in a way they had never done before. None of the participants had ever spoken about their experience as children of survivors, not even with long-time friends. "For many years I wanted to have such a discussion about second generation, but me and my friends never talked about it" (Itzik, dialogue participant). Even years later, people remarked on how strange it was that we never talked with one another about our experiences. The silence was finally over!

I also experienced the positive energy and a kind of lightness of being that happened when participants heard stories that they had in common; even stories that would seem bizarre or serious to someone else brought peals of laughter from those of us who had shared the same experience. One such example is a game Sylvia played with her brother. They would analyze the people who came and went in their home, and decided which of them would or would not survive a war. "My brother and I would often talk about the survivor traits, about people that we knew and family members. We would say: 'She

wouldn't have made it; nah, he would never make it; she would . . ."'
(Sylvia, dialogue participant).

When Sylvia shared this with the group, we all had a good laugh,
and then we proceeded to analyze each other: who would survive and
why, and who thought they would not survive. This was all particularly
intriguing, because I thought I had been alone in playing this rather
"sick" game. I would often analyze others according to their survivabil-
ity, but I also analyzed myself. I would imagine myself in the various
horrible situations: Would I tell the Nazis where someone was hiding if I
knew that I'd be killed for lying? Then I would judge myself badly, thinking that I would not be able to endure torture or the deaths of loved ones.
I would certainly give up and die. It didn't help that my mother would
regularly tell me that I was naïve and would never survive.

Our dialogue group also shared what we hadn't known and now
know about growing up as children of survivors. Pnina stated, "I didn't
realize while I was growing up, but after, I realized I am living in a
survival place. It's not the feeling of a child; it is the look of a grown up.
Now I know it is the living of a survivor. You don't need to buy something that isn't needed, just for fun."

The dialogues served to enable participants to talk openly about
emotions and experiences that that might have remained not only
unsaid but might have even remained in the unconscious. By speaking
about these, we were able to accept our reality without being overcome
by it, and in this way, to take important steps toward moving forward.

Dialogues are also a tool for building bridges between people
and for making collaborative decisions between citizens and governments or institutions, and with communities or ethnic groups.
America Speaks was a model of large-scale "Town Hall" dialogues
that invited all those who have a stake in an issue to participate in
public decision making, engaging hundreds or even thousands of
people in hundreds of places across the U.S. They shared experiences, considered a range of policy options, and decided together
what should be done. I was a volunteer Facilitator in one that was
held in New York at the Jacob Javitz Center to discuss the archi-

tectural plans for ground zero after the 2001 terrorist attacks. Over 5,000 people attended, with 200 volunteer Facilitators from around the world. At these sessions, America Speaks incorporated keypad polling and wireless networked computers into its meetings. It was also one of the first organizations to weave online discussion together with face-to-face meetings.

At the community level, there are many examples of successful dialogues. For example, Jewish–Arab dialogues in Givat Haviva are successfully building new relationships between these two communities in Israel.[13] The program has influenced other Israeli and Arab mayors to do the same. They have ensured the involvement of women, recognizing that women are key to social and economic change. Teenagers join in the dialogue in the hope that they will continue the dialogue at home. Their hope is to change the country and even the world.

The Parents Circle–Families Forum (PCFF) is a joint Palestinian–Israeli organization of over six hundred families, all of whom have lost a close family member as a result of the prolonged conflict. Joint activities have shown that reconciliation between individuals and nations is possible, and it is this insight that PCFF tries to pass on to both sides of the conflict. Moreover, the PCFF has concluded that the process of reconciliation between nations is a prerequisite to achieving a sustainable peace. The Parents Circle–Families Forum is registered as an association, and is managed jointly by a professional staff consisting of Israelis and Palestinians working in two offices: the Palestinian Office is at Beit Jala and the Israeli Office is in Ramat Ef'al, Tel Aviv.[14]

As mentioned earlier, in Mary Rothschild's emotional account, dialogues are ongoing between German Inheritors who suffer from terrible guilt and Jewish Inheritors who are appeased by the Germans' genuine sorrow, helping them let go of the guilt through assurances that they are not guilty. The documentary *What Our Fathers Did: A Nazi Legacy* makes the point that the children of Nazis are not accountable for the actions of their fathers, but they are obligated to recognize the truth of what happened.

There are Second, Third, and Fourth Generation Inheritors everywhere who find ways to educate future generations on intolerance and racism. What I am hoping to see are world-wide dialogues with Inheritors that will provide a means for processing and validating their deep sadness. Together Inheritors can bring meaning to their experiences and to their inherited memories, perhaps to their moral outrage and to the deep mourning that they have not been able to voice. This is what the dialogues have the potential to achieve—a kind of individual and generational re-orientation.

In Klee's drawing, perhaps the heavier lines are the burdens the children carry: a lost past, displacement and disaster, and perhaps, their own survivor parents. Without the roots of their past, the children's path has no strong foundation. The lighter lines, however, can be understood as their resilience, perhaps light enough to transcend the heaviness they bear.

The Positive Side of Moral Outrage

The only thing necessary for the triumph of evil is for good men to do nothing.

— Edmund Burke, Irish Statesman, political theorist, orator, author

There is a form of legitimate anger, i.e., moral outrage. I will discuss as a process that can be helpful for moving forward and appeasing our souls. To be clear, I am not talking about the kind of projective anger of an adolescent, or the entitled, close-minded attitude of extremists and religious zealots, or the defensiveness of victims (real or imagined) acting out aggressively. The kind of anger to which I refer—what I prefer to call moral or righteous outrage—is about the representation of suffering, not for the purpose of fighting but to reaffirm the moral principles of humanity.

Goodenough defines moral outrage as "[a] response to the behavior of others, never one's own. It is a response to infringements or transgressions on what people perceive to be the immunities they, or others with whom they identify, can expect on the basis of their rights and privileges and what they understand to be their reasonable expectations regarding the behavior of others."[15] He provides an interesting comparison with the animal world: Infringements of rights and privileges for humans are the equivalent of encroachments on territory among animals. Moral outrage can be understood as the human expression of territorial behavior in animals.

Wondering why mourning turns easily to anger, rage, or despair, I turned to my friend Quyhn-Tran with the question, "What is this anger that springs up so easily?" She wisely responded, "The rage is about remembering; if you forget, you have no anger." She knows this rage well, since the Vietnamese community is often treated as outsiders. She stressed that this type of anger is not a pathology. And I absolutely agree! For this reason, I use the term *moral outrage* to avoid confusing it with the destructive side of anger.

Kali Tal comments on the rebellious nature of the anger that bears witness to historical events in stubborn resistance to cover-ups or revisions: "Bearing witness is an aggressive act. It is born out of a refusal to bow to outside pressure to revise or to repress experience, a decision to embrace conflict rather than conformity, to endure a lifetime of anger and pain rather than to submit to the seductive pull of revision and repression. Its goal is change."[16]

I discovered the depth of my own outrage at Yad Vashem, the Holocaust Museum in Jerusalem. The first outrage came on learning was that the deaths of Hungarian Jews in the gas chambers could have, and really should have, been stopped. By 1944, what was happening in the death camps was well-known. Railway tracks and gas chambers could have been bombed and millions of lives saved. We still don't know what political decisions were at play then. The excuse I have heard is that these bombings would have hurt military strategies. I don't accept that. In fact, the Allies bombed the refineries just beside the gas chambers, so why didn't they bomb the gas chambers.

The second learning came from a moving, forty-nine-minute video testimony by documentarian Claude Lanzmann. He filmed the first eyewitness to the destruction of the Jews by Jan Karski, a Catholic Polish diplomat who served as an underground courier between Poland and the Polish government in exile. The tapes of Karski's accounts of his failed attempts to be listened to by the leaders of the free world are riveting and utterly devastating.[17]

Since the Polish government in exile was concerned with the internal politics of Poland's underground parties, Karski was assigned to meet with the different factions. When Karski met with two Jewish leaders, they appealed to him to see the situation for himself. In August 1942, with great risk to his life, he was smuggled into the Warsaw ghetto disguised in ragged clothes and wearing a Star of David. The entire population of around four hundred thousand were crammed into this area. He verified that what was being done to the Jews was even worse than he feared. He watched appalled as fourteen-year-old boys of the Hitler Youth—"all round, rosy-cheeked and blue-eyed"—hunted down human beings and killed them for sport. Here was a place where every semblance of decency, dignity, and humanity had gone.

A small part of his description: "Everyone seemed enveloped in a haze of disease and death. Children, every bone in their skeletons showing through their taut skins, played . . . 'They play before they die,' [Karski's] guide said, his voice breaking with emotion. 'I don't see many old people,' Karski whispered to the Jewish guide. 'Do they stay inside all day?' 'No,' said his guide, in a voice that seemed to issue from the grave. 'Don't you understand the German system yet? Those still capable of any effort are used for forced labor. The others are murdered by quota. They intend to kill us all.'"

Karski tried to take his message to Roosevelt, Churchill and other Allies, but he was met with disbelief and indifference. Current analysis explains that "his assessment probably did not sit happily with Allied leaders, who were even then doing a backdoor deal with Stalin, now their much-needed ally against Hitler, to hand a post-war Poland over to his sphere of influence. Karski, deeply anti-communist and determined that a free Poland would emerge from the wreckage of the war, was in danger of upsetting their carefully constructed apple cart for the future of eastern Europe. Poor Karski. He had two big warnings to give to the world—about Hitler's slaughter of the Jewish people and Stalin's evil intentions towards Poland. On both he was right, on both he was ignored, while others played politics with millions of lives."

On 2 June 1982, Yad Vashem recognized Jan Karski as *Righteous Among the Nations*. He died in 2002. In April 2012, President Barack Obama posthumously awarded the Presidential Medal of Freedom, the highest civilian award, to Jan Karski.[18]

If indifference and inaction wasn't enough reason for moral outrage, the final outrage came from the lack of fair administration of justice. It is outrageous that at the end of World War II, after having committed the worst crimes in the history of humankind, relatively few Germans were brought to trial for their crimes. Members of the Gestapo, the SS, and the Nazi party were accused and convicted. Twelve of the accused were sentenced to death, seven received prison sentences, and three were acquitted. None of the Third Reich's government, the general staff, or the commanders of the German army were executed. Many Nazi criminals returned to their jobs in the military as though nothing had happened.

There is an upside to moral outrage; it can be a motivator for positive change. Lieutenant General, Roméo Dallaire, who served as Force Commander for an unsupported mission (no arms, no military intervention allowed) to the United Nations Assistance Mission for Rwanda (UNAMIR) in 1993 and 1994, helplessly witnessed the country's descent into chaos and genocide of Rwanda's Tutsis, leading to deaths of more than 800,000 Rwandans, 300,000 of whom were children. His calls for help went unheeded. After this experience, General Dallaire suffered from severe PTSD, and tried to commit suicide. It is clear that moral outrage serves as a driver for retired General Dallaire to fight for just treatment of soldiers who suffer from PTSD. In the documentary *War in the Mind*, he ponders: "How do you change the culture of a conservative bastion of society that is also Darwinian in nature? If they don't see it, they've got a hard time understanding it. How do you handle them?" Dallaire answers his own question with the defiant and ethical act of moral outrage: "Well, you wear down the system. You just keep pummelling and pummelling and pummelling." Today we do call for international efforts to help people in jeopardy from civil wars, genocide, terror, and environmental disasters. That is the positive result of efforts by people like General Roméo Dallaire who express their moral outrage.

Without doubt, Inheritors may experience both the downside and the upside to anger and moral outrage. Hyper-vigilance to perceived or real injustice, rejection, or aggression is emotionally and physically exhausting. In addition, if one is overwhelmed by moral outrage, one may miss opportunities for inquiry and connection. It is important then to discern when anger is about being an agent for social change to address wrongs and to prevent future injustices, and not reactions to personal triggers.

Constructing Your Story

Chapter 11: Questions: Moving Forward

- Has your suffering, victimization and/or marginalization been acknowledged/validated?

- What have you been angry about—or more correctly, morally outraged about—that you have not been able to acknowledge adequately?

- How will you give voice to your feelings of outrage in a healthy way so that it isn't destructive to yourself or others?

- On a scale of 1-10, where is your pain now?

- What are your hopes as you move forward?

- What will you do to keep going, to make your hopes real?

12

A FINAL REFLECTION

A generation goes and a generation rises, but the earth remains forever. Also the sun rises and the sun sets; and hastening to its place it rises there again.

—Ecclesiastes 1:4-11

M y conversation with you began with a deep sense of sadness, but also with a determination to find a way to move forward from our inherited cherished burdens, our Inherited trauma. I have chosen to speak in terms of moving forward rather than moving on because moving on means forgetting a painful event and leaving it behind. Given that our burdens are cherished and we want to honor them, we don't want to forget them, but we do want to reclaim a life of our own that is joyful and light. There is no doubt we have had a heavy load to carry. I now think that it is possible that our burdens have actually helped us to move forward. What I first saw as an unhealthy enmeshment of parents and children, I can now see as a supportive and a generative sharing of their resilient spirit with us.

At this point, I must confess I was concerned that we have already heard so much about the Holocaust that readers might not be interested in this book. I hope I have shown that we can indeed talk specifically as well as universally about the Holocaust, about all trauma, and about the trans-generational impacts of traumatic events as common experiences. As I have emphasized throughout this book, the silence, the *not-speaking*, is the most dangerous threat to our well-being and to the well-being of our descendants.

I hope that we collectively acknowledge the challenges faced by Inheritors of trauma. There are important lessons to be learned, lessons that can support the preservation of humanity.

After all of these studies, it seems that the most important things we can do are also the most obvious. We need to help mothers and fathers care for their children from infancy onwards, so that children are able to find healthy self-soothing practices as they grow up. We need to help parents understand that their own needs are not the responsibility of their children; and what we all know, but don't always practice, is that the love and the protection of our children are the most important of all.

The lines in the *Burdened Children* drawing, lines that seem to have no beginning and no end point, are our beginning points for new conversations and new journeys. The drawing depicts only two thin legs that must carry a large load while rebuilding a life and carrying on. Perhaps continuing the dialogue that began here will help share their load and add some walking-power!

Perhaps by finding a renewed voice we can give the Klee children mouths, where there are none!

I look forward to ongoing dialogues with Inheritors of past and current tragedies and devastation, and with anyone interested in pursuing some of the possibilities surfaced in this work.

For those of you who want to process your own story and find you own voice, I would encourage you to bring a group of people together, have a conversation, share stories, and spend time with each other. Trust that it will work. Please write to me on my website, www.gitabaack.com, and tell me what happens when you do this. Feel free to send pictures, drawings, poems, etc.

As I close, I discover yet another epiphany. I realize that, in using Klee's drawing, I have chosen an image of children, because it provides a representation of my brother and my sister. In this writing, and in the writing of so many people, we are honoring the memory and maintaining the visibility of our lost families and ancestors. Of course we are resilient! We have a precious legacy to carry!

Helena and Henush thank you for accompanying me on this walk. Thank you for our profound and everlasting connection. Thank you for the honor of loving you.

Constructing Your Story

Chapter 12: Questions: A Final Reflection

I hope that you have been able to complete some of the unfinished business of your soul. These final questions aim to help you make that final shift towards a lighter future.

- What do you see in the Klee drawing that you didn't see at the beginning?

- How can you honor your own cherished legacy?

- Visualize yourself living a life with a new calmness and compassion for your ancestors, yourself, and others. This is a vision of your ideal life. Describe in detail what a typical day looks like: what you are doing, who are you with, where do you live, and so on.

- Write a letter to yourself or to someone who is important to you, and talk about what kind of support you need to keep you going on your new path.

PERMISSIONS

Artwork

Belastete Kinder (Burdened Children) 1930, by Paul Klee, Swiss, 1879–1940
Licensed from the Tate Gallery, London, U.K.
Graphite, crayon and ink on paper on board
Support: 65x458 mm

Acquired by the Tate Gallery, London, U.K., bequeathed by Elly Kahnweiler 1991 to form part of the gift of Gustav and Elly Kahnweiler accessioned 1994.

Angelus Novus (Angel of History) 1920, by Paul Klee, Swiss, 1879–1940
Courtesy of The Israel Museum, Jerusalem
Oil transfer and watercolor on paper, 318x242 mm

Gift of Fania and Gershom Scholem, Jerusalem, John Herring, Marlene and Paul Herring, Jo-Carole and Ronald Lauder, New York, to The Israel Museum, Jerusalem. B87.0994

Photo © The Israel Museum, Jerusalem, by Elie Posner

Photographs

Personal collection, Gita Arian Baack

Films and Documentaries
FILMS

The Diary of Anne Frank (George Stevens, 1959)
Deconstructing Harry (Woody Allen, 1997)
Defiance (Pieter Jan Brugge, 2008)
Fugitive Pieces (Robert Lantos, 2007)
Gentleman's Agreement (Darryl F. Zanuck, 1947)
Holocaust (TV mini-series, Robert Berger, 1978)
Munich (Steven Spielberg, 2005)
The Pawnbroker (Sidney Lumet, 1964)
The Pianist (Roman Polanski, 2002)
Schindler's List (Steven Spielberg, 1994)
Sophie's Choice (Alan J. Pakula, 1982)
Twelve Years a Slave (Steve McQueen, 2013)
The Young Lions (Al Lichtman, 1958)

DOCUMENTARIES

The Official Story/La Historia Oficial (*The Dirty War;*
   Luis Puenzo, Argentina, 1985)
The Partisans of Vilna: The Untold Story of Jewish Resistance
   (Aviva Kempner, 2005)
Shoah (Claude Lanzmann, 1985)
War in the Mind (Judy Jackson, Betsy Carson, 2011)
What Our Fathers Did: A Nazi Legacy (David Evans, 2015)
When the Boys Come Home (Absolutely Canadian CBC
   documentary series, Mike Wert, 2015)
The World was Ours (Mira Jednwabnik Van Doren, 2005)

NOTES

Chapter 2:

1. The information in this section is available on the Genocide Watch website http://genocidewatch.net/genocide/.
2. Timothy Snyder, *Black Earth: The Holocaust as History and Warning* (New York: Tim Duggan Books, 2015), xii-xiii.
3. Truth and Reconciliation Commission of Canada, *Honouring the Truth, Reconciling for the Future: Summary of the Final Report of the Truth and Reconciliation Commission of Canada* (Toronto: The Truth and Reconciliation Commission of Canada, 2015), www.trc.ca/websites/trcinstitution/File/2015/Findings/Exec_Summary _2015_05_31_web_o.pdf.
4. Jesse Staniforth, "'Cultural Genocide'? No, Canada committed regular genocide," *The Toronto Star*, June 10, 2015, https://www.thestar.com/opinion/commentary/2015/06/10/cultural-genocide-no-canada-committed-regular-genocide.html.
5. David E. Stannard, *American Holocaust: The Conquest of the New World* (New York: Oxford University Press, 1992), xi.
6. Judith Shulevitz, "The Science of Suffering," *New Republic*, Nov 16, 2014, https://newrepublic.com/article/120144/trauma-genetic-scientists-say-parents-are-passing-ptsd-kids.

7.   Maria Brave Heart and Lemyra M. DeBruyn, "The American Indian Holocaust: Healing Historical Unresolved Grief," *American Indian and Alaska Native Mental Health Research* 8, no. 2 (1998): 60-82.

8.   Retrieved from website http://abhmuseum.org/what-is-the-black-holocaust/.

9.   Retrieved from website http://eji.org/enslavement-to-mass-incarceration-museum

10. Tyrone Wilson, "From Enslavement to Mass Incarceration, in *Black Lives Matter* https://blackmattersus.com/9820-from-enslavement-to-mass-incarceration/.

11. Jessica Henderson Daniel, "The Courage to Hear: African American Women's Memories of Racial Trauma," in *Psychotherapy with African American Women: Innovations in Psychodynamic Perspectives and Practice,* ed. Leslie C. Jackson and Beverly Greene (New York: The Guilford Press, 2004), 134.

12. Ibid., 129.

13. Ibid., 131.

14. Ibid., 135-145.

15. Samuel R. Aymer, "I Can't Breathe: A Case Study—Helping Black Men Cope With Race-Related Trauma Stemming From Police Killing And Brutality," *Journal of Human Behavior in the Social Environment* 26, no. 3-4, 367-376.

Chapter 3:

1. Florabel Kinsler, "Second Generation Effects of the Holocaust: The Effectiveness of Group Therapy in the Resolution of the Transmission of Parental Trauma," *Journal of Psychology and Judaism* 6, no. 1 (1981): 53-67.

2. Christopher Fortune, "The analytic nursery: Ferenczi's 'wise baby' meets Jung's 'divine child'," *The Journal of Analytical Psychology* 48, no. 4 (2003): 457-466.

Chapter 4:

1. Kenneth Gergen, *Relational Being: Beyond Self and Community*, (New York: Oxford University Press, 2009).

2. Retrieved from "On the Jewish Question," in *Posen speeches*, https://en.wikipedia.org/wiki/Posen_speeches.

3. Timothy Snyder, *Black Earth: The Holocaust as History and Warning* (New York: Tim Duggan Books, 2015), 166-190.

4. Carol A. Kidron, "Embracing the Lived Memory of Genocide: Holocaust Survivor and Descendant Renegade Memory Work at the House of Being," *Journal of the American Ethnological Society* 37, no. 3 (2010): 6.

5. Snyder, *Black Earth*, 201.

6. Alice Miller, *The Drama of the Gifted Child: The Search for the True Self* (New York: Basic Books, 1981), 27.

7. Esther Rashkin, "The Haunted Child: Social Catastrophe, Phantom Transmissions, and the Aftermath of Collective Trauma," *Psychoanalytic Review* 86, no. 3 (1999): 3.

8. Esther Rashkin, *Unspeakable Secrets and the Psychoanalysis of Culture* (Albany: State University of New York Press, 2008), 105.

9. Ibid., 20.

10. Ibid., 52.

11. Ibid.

12. Ibid., 107-109.

13. Ibid., 109-111.

14. Ann Parry, 'To give death a place'—Rejecting the 'ineffability' of the Holocaust: the work of Gillian Rose and Anne Michaels," Journal of European Studies 30:120 (2000): 353–368

15. Judith Shulevitz, "The Science of Suffering," *New Republic*, Nov 16, 2014, https://newrepublic.com/article/120144/trauma-genetic-scientists-say-parents-are-passing-ptsd-kids.

16. Rosanna Deerchild, "Trauma Research Brings Pain, Healing to Academic Jesse Thistle," *CBC Radio—Unreserved*, December 6, 2015, http://www.cbc.ca/radio/unreserved/taking-the-first-steps-on-the-

road-to-reconciliation-1.3347611/trauma-research-brings-pain-heal-ing-to-academic-jesse-thistle-1.3350632.

17. Marianne Hirsch, "Past Lives: Postmemories in Exile," in *Poetics Today* 17, no. 4 (1996): 663.

18. Ibid., 559.

19. Stefan Goebel, "Beyond Discourse? Bodies and Memories of Two World Wars," *Journal of Contemporary History* 42 (2007): 377.

20. Alice Miller, *The Drama of the Gifted Child*, 21.

21. Ibid.

Chapter 5:

1. Anna Mieszkowska, *Irena Sendler: Mother of the Children of the Holocaust* (England: Oxford, 2011), 149-150.

2. Miep Gies and Alison Leslie Gold, *Anne Frank Remembered: The Story of the Woman Who Helped to Hide the Frank Family* (New York: Simon & Schuster Paperbacks, 2009), 9.

3. Retrieved from: "Being Anne Frank's Best Friend," June 5-11, 2015, http://printarchive.epochtimes.com/a1/en/us/nyc/2015/06/05_Epoch%20Weekend/AF06.pdf

4. Martin Gilbert, *The Righteous—The Unsung Heroes of the Holocaust* (London: Doubleday, 2002), 88.

5. A PDF of the exhibition can be retrieved from www.vhec.org/images/pdfs/Muslim%20Rescuers%20Teachers%20Guide.pdf.

6. Herbert Pundik, *In Denmark It Could Not Happen: The Flight of the Jews to Sweden in 1943* (Jerusalem: Gefen, 1998), 134.

7. Timothy Snyder, *Black Earth: The Holocaust as History and Warning* (New York: Tim Duggan Books, 2015), 257-259.

8. Interviews with Abba Kovner www.ushmm.org/online/film/display/detail.php?file_num=5010&clip_id=23D2ADDF-645B-4AD9-9D0A-DFF1159D7A66.

9. Retrieved from http://chgs.umn.edu/museum/responses/hergeth/bio.html.

10. Aviva Ravel, *Faithful Unto Death: The Story of Arthur Zygielbaum* (Montreal: Arthur Zygielbaum Branch, Workmen's Circle, 1980).

11. Retrieved from Wikipedia, https://en.wikipedia.org/wiki/The_Little _Smuggler.

12. Horst Biesold, *Crying Hands: Eugenics and Deaf People in Nazi Germany* (Washington: Gaulladet University Press, 2004).

13. Sonja M. Hedgepeth and Rochelle G. Saidel, *Sexual Violence against Jewish Women during the Holocaust* (Waltham: Brandeis Press, 2010), ix.

14. Jessica Ravitz, "Silence lifted: The untold stories of rape during the Holocaust," *CNN*, June 24, 2011, http://www.cnn.com/2011/ WORLD/europe/06/24/holocaust.rape/.

15. Retrieved from https://en.wikipedia.org/wiki/Comfort_women.

16. Retrieved from http://survivors-fund.org.uk/resources/rwandan-history/statistics/.

17. The official website for the International Tracing Service is: www. its-arolsen.org/en/.

Chapter: 6

1. Jessica Henderson Daniel, "The Courage to Hear: African American Women's Memories of Racial Trauma," in *Psychotherapy with African American Women: Innovations in Psychodynamic Perspectives and practice,* ed. Leslie C. Jackson and Beverly Greene (New York: Guilford Press, 2000), 136.

2. Harriet Lerner, *Dance of Intimacy* (New York, Harper and Row, 1989), 28-117.

3. Alice Miller, *The Drama of the Gifted Child: The Search for the True Self* (New York: Basic Books, 1981), 43-86.

4. Dan Bar-On, *Fear and Hope: Three Generations of the Holocaust* (Cambridge: Harvard University Press, 1998), 319-32

5. Miller, *The Drama of the Gifted Child*, 85-86.

6. Dina Wardi, *Memorial Candles: Children of the Holocaust* (New York: Routledge, 1992), 102.

Chapter 7:

1. Natan F. Kellermann, "Diagnosis of Holocaust Survivors and their Children," *Israel Journal of Psychiatry and Related Sciences* 36, no. 1 (1999), 57.
2. Ibid., 63.
3. Dina Wardi, *Memorial Candles: Children of the Holocaust* (New York: Routledge: 1992).
4. Dan Bar-On, "Multigenerational Perspectives on Coping with the Holocaust Experience: An Attachment Perspective for Understanding the Developmental Sequelae of Trauma across Generations," in *International Journal of Behavioral Development* Vol. 22 No. 2 (1998), 315–338
5. Roger S. Gottlieb, *Thinking the Unthinkable: Meanings of the Holocaust* (New Jersey: Paulist Press, 1990), 390.
6. Dan Bar-On, *Fear and Hope: Three Generations of the Holocaust* (Cambridge: Harvard University Press, 1998).
7. Janet Geringer Woititz, *Adult Children of Alcoholics* (Deerfield Beach: Health Communications, Inc., 1983).
8. Wardi, "Memorial Candles," 25.
9. Dan Bar-On, "Multigenerational Perspectives," 325.
10. Faiga Burman Wajcer and Simon Wajcer, *So You Can Tell: Prisoner 48378 Auschwitz* (Montreal: White Sir Press, 2014).
11. Carol Kidron, "Toward an Ethnography of Silence: The Lived Presence of the Past in the Everyday Life of Holocaust Survivors and their Descendants in Israel," *Current Anthropology* 50, no. 1 (2009), 13.
12. Elie Wiesel, *After the Darkness: Reflections on the Holocaust* (New York: Schocken Books, 2002), 47.
13. Mary H. Rothschild, "Transforming Our Legacies: Heroic Journeys for Children of Nazi Perpetrators," *Journal of Humanistic Psychology* 40, no. 3 (2002), 51.
14. Rothschild, "Transforming Our Legacies," 43-44.
15. Kate Connolly, "*Being German is a huge burden*," in *The Guardian*,

Berlin, September 16 2012, https://www.theguardian.com/world/2012 /sep/16/bernhard-schlink-germany-burden-euro-crisis.

16. Rothschild, "Transforming Our Legacies," 47-50.

17. Ibid., 47

18. Ibid., 49-50.

19. Ibid., 51.

20. Simon Wiesenthal, *The Sunflower* (New York: Schocken Books, 1998).

Chapter 8:

1. Victor E. Frankl, *Man's Search for Meaning* (New York: Beacon Press 1962).

2. Ibid., 112.

3. David Samuels, "Do Jews Carry Trauma In Our Genes? A Conversation With Rachel Yehuda," *Tablet*, December 11, 2014, http://www.tabletmag.com/jewish-arts-and-culture/books/187555/trauma-genes-q-a-rachel-yehuda.

4. Roni Berger and Tzipi Weiss, "The Posttraumatic Growth Model: An Expansion to the Family System," *Traumatology* 15, no. 1 (2009), 63-74, doi: 10.1177/1534765608323499, http://tmt.sagepub.com.

5. Zieva Konvisser, *Living Beyond Terrorism: Israeli Stories of Hope and Healing* (Jerusalem, Gefen Publishing House, 2014), 47.

6. Ibid., 106.

7. Ibid., 54.

8. Ibid., 159.

9. Dan Senor and Saul Singer, *Start-up Nation: The Story of Israel's Economic Miracle* (New York: Twelve—Hachette Book Group, 2009), 30.

10. John J. Sigal, "Resilience in Survivors, Their Children and Their Grandchildren," in *Echoes of the Holocaust* 4, ed. Shalom Robinson (1995),

11. Elie Wiesel, *After the Darkness: Reflections on the Holocaust* (New York: Schocken Books, 2002), 12-13.

12. Richard Raskin, *Life is Like a Glass of Tea: Studies of Classic Jewish Jokes* (Aarhus: Aarhus University Press, 1992), 79.

13. Franklin Littell, "After Forty Years in the Wilderness, The Unfinished Agenda," *Journal of Ecumenical Studies* 46, no. 4 (2011), 3.

Chapter 9:

1. Retrieved from: www.integrativepro.com/Resources/Integrative-Blog/2016/General-Adaptation-Syndrome-Stages.

2. Tori Rodriguez, "Descendants of Holocaust Survivors Have Altered Stress Hormones," *Scientific American* 26, no. 2, February 12, 2015, https://www.scientificamerican.com/article/descendants-of-holocaust-survivors-have-altered-stress-hormones/.

3. Mary Annette Pember, "Trauma May Be Woven Into DNA of Native Americans," *Indian Country Today Media Network*, May 28, 2015, http://indiancountrytodaymedianetwork.com/2015/05/28/trauma-may-be-woven-dna-native-americans-160508).

4. Retrieved from a *New York Times* article, titled "A Pregnancy Souvenir: Cells that are not Your Own," www.nytimes.com/2015/09/15/science/a-pregnancy-souvenir-cells-that-are-not-your-own.html?_r=0D.

5. Daniel Goleman, "The Brain and Emotional Intelligence: An Interview with Daniel Goleman," *tricycle*, May 18, 2011, http://tricycle.org/trikedaily/brain-and-emotional-intelligence-interview-daniel-goleman/.

Chapter 10:

1. Zygmunt Bauman, *Modernity and the Holocaust* (New York: Cornell University Press, 1989), 50-65.

2. Claude Lanzmann, *Shoah: An Oral History of the Holocaust, the Complete Text of the Film* (New York: Pantheon Books, 1985), xvii.

3. Christopher Browning, preface to *Ordinary Men: Reserve Police Battalion 101 and the Final Solution in Poland* (New York: Harper Collins, 1998), xvi.

4. Ibid., xvii.

5. Ibid., 186.

6. Ibid.,188-189.

Chapter 11:

1. Deborah E. Lipstadt, *The Eichmann Trial* (New York: Schocken Books, 2011), 24.

2. Ibid., 25.

3. Mary Field Belenky, *Women's Ways of Knowing: The Development of Self, Voice and Mind* (New York: Basic Books, 1997).

4. Tom Segev, *The Seventh Million: The Israelis and the Holocaust* (New York: Holt Paperbacks, 1991), 11.

5. Retrieved from www.kayentatownship-nsn.gov/blog/?p=7095.

6. Retrievedfromhttp://jamaica-gleaner.com/article/news/20151008/full-text-pj-slams-david-cameron-are-we-not-worthy-he-asks.

7. Retrieved from www.rogerebert.com/reviews/great-movie-shoah-1985.

8. Ibid.

9. Eckhart Tolle, *A New Earth: Awakening to Your Life's Purpose* (New York: Penguin Books, 2005), 159.

10. Ibid., 144-145.

11. Janusz Korczak, *Loving Every Child: Wisdom for Parents* (Chapel Hill: Algonquin Books, 2007), 2.

12. Harlene Anderson, *Conversation, Language, and Possibilities: A Postmodern Approach to Therapy* (New York: Basic Books, 1997), 115-116.

13. Retrieved from www.youtube.com/user/ronitghsec.

14. Retrieved from www.theparentscircle.com/Content.aspx?ID=2#.
V7ew_ZMrKgQ0.

15. Ward H. Goodenough, "Moral Outrage: Territoriality in Human
Guise," *Zygon: Journal of Religion and Science* 32, no. 1 (1997), 5.

16. Kali Tal, *Worlds of Hurt: Reading the Literatures of Trauma* (Cambridge: Cambridge University Press, 1996), 7.

17. Retrieved from www.yadvashem.org/yv/en/righteous/stories/kar-
ski.asp.

18. Retrieved from www.ushmm.org/online/film/display/detail.php?-
file_num=4739.

19. "The Ethics Of Using Medical Data From Nazi Experiments," can
be found on www.jlaw.com/Articles/NaziMedEx.html.

BIBLIOGRAPHY

Abella, Irving, and Harold Martin Troper. *None is Too Many: Canada and the Jews of Europe 1933–1948*. Toronto: University of Toronto Press, 2012.

Abrams, Harry N. *Paul Klee 1879–1940*. Cologne, West Germany: Abrams and Schauberg, 1969.

Anderson, Harlene. *Conversation, Language, and Possibilities: A Postmodern Approach to Therapy*. Basic Books, New York, N.Y., 1997.

Arian Baack, Gita. *An Exploration of Resilience in the Generation After the Holocaust: Implications for Secondary Inheritors of Trauma, Displacement and Disastrous Events*. PhD dissertation, Tilburg University: The Netherlands, 2012.

Aymer, Samuel R. "I Can't Breathe: A Case Study—Helping Black Men Cope with Race-Related Trauma Stemming from Police Killing and Brutality." *Journal of Human Behavior in the Social Environment* 26:3–4 (2016): 367–376.

Bar-On, Dan. *Fear and Hope: Three Generations of the Holocaust*. Cambridge: Harvard University Press, 1995.

Bar-On, Dan. *The Indescribable and the Undiscussable: Reconstructing Human Discourse after Trauma*. Budapest: Central European University Press, 1999.

Bar-On, Dan, et al. "Multigenerational Perspectives on Coping with the Holocaust Experience: An Attachment Perspective for Understanding the Developmental Sequelae of Trauma across Generations" *International Journal of Behavioral Development* 22:2 (1998): 315–338.

Bauman, Zygmunt. *Modernity and The Holocaust*. Ithaca: Cornell University Press, 1989.

Belenky, Mary Field. *Women's Ways of Knowing: The Development of Self, Voice and Mind*. New York: Basic Books, 1986.

Belsky, Jay. "War, Trauma and Children's Development: Observations from a Modern Evolutionary Perspective." *International Journal of Behavioural Development* 32:4 (2008): 260–271.

Benjamin, Walter. *Theses on the Philosophy of History*. New York: Random House, 2011.

Berger, Alan L. *Children of Job: American Second-Generation Witnesses to the Holocaust*. Albany: State University of New York Press, 1997.

Berger, Alan and Naomi Berger. *Second Generation Voices: Reflections by Children of the Holocaust*. Syracuse, NY: Syracuse University Press, 2001.

Berger, Roni and Tzipi Weiss. "The Posttraumatic Growth Model: An Expansion to the Family System," *Traumatology* 15:1 (2009): 63–74.

Biesold, Horst. *Crying Hands: Eugenics and Deaf People in Nazi Germany.* Washington, DC: Gaulladet University Press, 2004.

Blum, Harold P. "Psychic Trauma and Traumatic Object Loss." *Journal of the American Psychoanalytic Association* 51:2 (2003), 415–432.

Brave Heart, Maria Yellow Horse & Lemyra M. DeBruyn. "The American Indian Holocaust: Healing Historical Unresolved Grief." *American Indian and Alaska Native Mental Health Research* 8:2 (1998): 56–78.

Browning, Christopher. *Ordinary Men: Reserve Police Battalion 101 and The Final Solution in Poland.* New York: Harper Collins, 1993.

Bulka, Reuven P. *Holocaust Aftermath: Continuing impact on the Generations.* Human Sciences Press, 1981.

Burman, Faiga and Simon Wajcer. *So You Can Tell: Prisoner 48378 Auschwitz.* Montreal: White Sir Press, 2004.

Caruth, Cathy. *Trauma: Exploration in Memory.* Baltimore: Johns Hopkins University Press, 1995.

Daniel, Jessica Henderson. "The Courage to Hear: African American Women's Memories of Racial Trauma." In *Psychotherapy with African American Women: Innovations in Psychodynamic Perspectives and Practice,* edited by Leslie C. Jackson and Beverly Greene. New York: The Guilford Press, 2000.

Danieli, Yael. *International Handbook of Multigenerational Legacies of Trauma.* New York: Springer Science & Business Media, 1998.

Dasberg, Haim. "Psychological distress of Holocaust survivors and offspring in Israel, forty years later: A review." *Israel Journal of Psychiatry and Related Sciences* 24 (1987): 243–256.

David, Paula. "Issues of Death and Dying for Adult Children of Holocaust Survivors." Presentation to the Council of Social Work Education, Atlanta, 2003.

Deerchild, Rosanna. "Trauma Research Brings Pain, Healing to Academic Jesse Thistle," *CBC Radio—Unreserved*, December 6, 2015, http://www.cbc.ca/radio/unreserved/taking-the-first-steps-on-the-road-to-reconciliation-1.3347611/trauma-research-brings-pain-healing-to-academic-jesse-thistle-1.3350632.

Degruy, Joy Angela. *Post Traumatic Slave Syndrome: America's Legacy of Enduring Injury and Healing*. Portland, OR: Joy Degruy Publishing, 2005.

Denham, Aaron R. "Rethinking Historical Trauma: Narratives of Resilience." *Transcultural Psychiatry* 45:3 (2008), 391–414.

Ellis, Carolyn. "Telling Secrets, Revealing Lives: Relational Ethics in Research with Intimate Others." *Qualitative Inquiry* 13:1 (2007): 3–29.

Epstein, Helen. *Children of the Holocaust: Conversations with Sons and Daughters of Survivors*. New York: Penguin Books, 1979.

Fleming, J. and R.J. Ledogar. "Resilience, an Evolving Concept: a Review of Literature Relevant to Aboriginal Research." *Pimativsiwin: A Journal of Aboriginal and Indigenous Community Health*, 6:2 (2008): 7–23.

Fortune, Christopher. "The analytic nursery: Ferenczi's 'wise baby' meets Jung's 'divine child'," *The Journal of Analytical Psychology* 48:4 (2003): 457–466.

Foucault, Michel. *Power/Knowledge: Selected Interviews and Other Writings 1972-1977*. Brighton: Harvester Press, 1980.

Frank, Anne. *The Diary of a Young Girl, Definitive Edition*. New York: Anchor/ Doubleday, 1991.

Frankl, Victor E. *Man's Search for Meaning*. New York: Beacon Press, 1962.

Frankl, Victor E , Elie Weisel, Primo Levi, Jerzy Kozinski. "Voices of the Wise and Troubled." *Journal of Psychology and Judaism* 6:1 (1981).

Fredman, Glenda. *Transforming Emotion: Conversations in Counselling and Psychotherapy*. London: Whurr Publishers, 2004.

Gies, Miep, and Alison Leslie Gold. *Anne Frank Remembered: The Story of the Woman Who Helped to Hide the Frank Family*. New York: Simon & Schuster, 1988.

Gergen, Kenneth J. and M. Gergen. *Social Construction: Entering the Dialogue*. Chagrin Falls, Ohio: Taos Institute Publications, 2004.

Gergen, Kenneth J. *Relational Being: Beyond Self and Community*. New York: Oxford University Press, 2009.

Gilbert, Martin. *The Righteous—The Unsung Heroes of the Holocaust*. London: Doubleday, 2002.

Goebel, Stefan, et al.. "Beyond Discourse? Bodies and Memories of Two World Wars." *Journal of Contemporary History* 42 (2007), 377–385.

Goleman, Daniel. "The Brain and Emotional Intelligence: An Interview with Daniel Goleman," *tricycle*, May 18, 2011, http://tricycle.org/ trikedaily/brain-and-emotional-intelligence-interview-daniel-goleman/.

Goodenough, Ward H. "Moral Outrage: Territoriality in Human Guise." *Zygon: Journal of Religion and Science* 32:1 (March 1997): 5–28.

Gottlieb, Rogers. *Thinking the Unthinkable: Meanings of the Holocaust.* Mahwah, NJ: Paulist Press, 1990.

Haftman, Werner. *The Mind and Work of Paul Klee.* New York: Praeger, 1954.

Hass, Aaron. *In The Shadow Of The Holocaust: The 2nd Generation.* Cambridge: Cambridge University Press, 1996.

Hawley, Dale R., and Laura De Haan. (1996) "Toward a definition of family resilience: Integrating life-span and family perspectives." *Family Process*, 35:3 (1996): 283–298.

Hedgepeth, Sonja M. and Rochelle G. Saidel, eds. *Sexual Violence against Jewish Women during the Holocaust.* Lebanon, NH: Brandeis University Press, 2010.

Hirsch, Marianne. "Past Lives: Postmemories in Exile." *Poetics Today*, 17:4 (1996), 659–686.

Hirsch, Marianne. *Family frames: Photography, Narrative, and Postmemory.* Cambridge: Harvard University Press, 1997.

Hoffman, Eva. *After Such Knowledge: Memory, History and the Aftermath of the Holocaust.* New York: Public Affairs Press, 2004.

Hogman, Flora. "Resilience in Survivors, Their Children and Their Grandchildren." *Echoes of the Holocaust* 6 (2000).

Ijzendoorn, Marinus H., et al. "Multigenerational Perspective on Coping with the Holocaust Experience: An Attachment Perspective for Understanding the Developmental Sequelae of Trauma across Generations." *International Journal of Behavioural Development* 22:2 (1998), 315–338.

Jung, C.G.*The Undiscovered Self: The Dilemma of The Individual In Modern Society.* New York: New American Library, 2006.

Kangisser Cohen, Sharon. "The Experience of the Jewish Family in the Nazi Ghetto: Kovno—A Case Study." *Journal of Family History* 31: 3 (2006), 267–288.

Kaplan, Howard B. "Toward an understanding of resilience: A critical review of definitions and models," in M.D. Glantz and J.L. Johnson, eds., *Resilience and development: Positive life adaptations.* New York: Kluwer Academic/Plenum, 1999.

Karlen, Neal. *The Story of Yiddish: How a Mish-Mosh of Languages Saved the Jews.* New York: HarperCollins, 2009.

Keats, Patrice A. "Vicarious Witnessing in European Concentration Camps: Imagining the Trauma of Another." *Traumatology* 11:3 (2005): 171.

Kellerman, Natan P.F. "Diagnosis of Holocaust Survivors and Their Children." *Israel Journal of Psychiatry and Related Sciences* 36:1 (1999): 56–65.

Kellerman, Natan P.F. "Transmission of Holocaust Trauma: An Integrative View." *Psychiatry* 64:3 (2001): 256–267.

Kellerman, Natan P.F. "Psychopathology in Children of Holocaust Survivors: A Review of the Literature." *Israel Journal of Psychiatry and Related Sciences* 38:1 (2001), 36–46.

Kestenberg, Judith S. "Children of Survivors and Child Survivors." *Echoes of the Holocaust* 1 (1992): 27–50.

Kidron, Carol A. "Embracing the Lived Memory of Genocide: Holocaust Survivor and Descendant Renegade Memory Work at the House of Being." *American Ethnologist* 37:3 (2010), 429-451.

Kidron, Carol A. "In Pursuit of Jewish Paradigms of Memory: Con-
    stituting Carriers of Jewish Memory in a Support Group for Chil-
    dren of Holocaust Survivors." *Dapim: Studies on the Holocaust* 23:1
    (2009): 7–43.

Kidron, Carol A. "Toward an Ethnography of Silence: The Lived Pres-
    ence of the Past in Everyday Life of Holocaust Survivors and their
    Descendants in Israel." *Current Anthropology* 50:1 (2009): 5–27.

King, Anthony P., Jennifer N. Leichtman, James L. Ableson, Israel
    Liverzon, and Julia S. Seng. "Ecological Salivary Cortisol Analysis
    Part 2: Relative Impact of Trauma History, Posttraumatic Stress,
    Comorbidity, Chronic Stress, and Known Confounds on Hor-
    mone Levels." *Journal of the American Psychiatric Nurses Associa-
    tion* 14:4 (2008), 285–296.

Kinsler, Florabel. "Second generation of the Holocaust: The effectiveness
    of group therapy in the resolution of the transmission of parental
    trauma." *Journal of Psychology and Judaism* 6:1 (1981), 53–67.

Klein, Melanie and Joan Riviere. *Love, Hate and Reparation.* New York:
    W.W. Norton and Co., 1964.

Konvisser, Zieva. *Living Beyond Terrorism.* Jerusalem: Gefen Publish-
    ing House, Ltd., 2014.

Korczak, Janusz. *Loving Every Child: Wisdom for Parents.* Chapel Hill,
    NC: Algonquin Books, 2007.

Kuperstein, Elana Eizak. "Adolescents of Parent Survivors of Concen-
    tration Camps: A Review of the Literature." *Journal of Psychology
    and Judaism* 6:1 (1981).

Lafrance, J., et al. "Synchronicity or Serendipity? Aboriginal Wisdom and Childhood Resilience." In L. and M. Liebenberg, eds., *Resilience in Action*. Toronto: University of Toronto Press (2008), 289–320.

Lanzmann, Claude. *Shoah: An Oral History of the Holocaust, the Complete Text of the Film*. New York: Pantheon Books, 1985.

Lerner, Harriet. *Dance of Intimacy*. New York: Harper and Row, 1989.

Lev-Wiesel, Rachel. "Intergenerational Transmission of Trauma across Three Generations." *Qualitative Social Work* 6:1 (2007): 75–94.

Leventhal, Robert S. "Romancing the Holocaust, or Hollywood and Horror: Steven Spielberg's *Schindler's List*." Department of German, University of Virginia, 1995.

Lindern, Evelin Gerda. "Humiliation Trauma That Has Been Overlooked: An Analysis Based on Fieldwork in Germany, Rwanda/Burundi, and Somalia." *Traumatology* 7:1 (2001): 43–68.

Lipstadt, Deborah E. *The Eichmann Trial*. New York: Next Book/Schocken, 2011.

Littell, Franklin. "After Forty Years in the Wilderness, The Unfinished Agenda." *Journal of Ecumenical Studies* 46:4 (2011): 479.

Major, Ellinor E. "The Impact of the Holocaust on the Second Generation: Norwegian Jewish Holocaust Survivors and their Children." *Journal of Traumatic Stress* 9:3 (1996): 441–454.

Masten, Ann S., Karin M. Best and Norman Garmezy. "Resilience and Development: Contributions from the study of children who overcome adversity." *Development and Psychopathology* 2:4 (1990), 425–444.

Maxfield, Louise, Kristine Lake and Lee Hyer. "Some Answers to Unanswered Questions about the Empirical Support for EMDR in the Treatment of PTSD." *Traumatology* 10:73 (2004).

McAdam-Crisp, Jacqueline L. "Factors that can Enhance and Limit Resilience for Children of War." *Childhood* 13:4 (2006): 459–477.

McAlister, Sean. "'The explosive devices of memory': trauma and the construction of identity in narrative." *Language and Literature* 15:1 (2006): 91-106.

Michaels, Anne. *Fugitive Pieces.* Toronto: McClelland and Stewart, 1996.

Mieszkowska, Anna. *Irena Sendler: Mother of the Children of the Holocaust.* Oxford, England, 2011.

Miller, Alice. *The Drama of the Gifted Child: The Search for the True Self.* 3rd ed. New York: Basic Books, 2007.

Miller, Alice. *From Rage to Courage.* New York: W.W. Norton and Co., 2009.

Monk, Gerald, John Winslade, Kathie Crocket, and David Epston. *Narrative Therapy in Practice.* San Francisco: Jossey-Bass, 1997.

Nhat Hahn, Thich. *Peace is Every Step: The Path of Mindfulness In Everyday Life.* Bantam Books, 1991.

Parry, Ann. "'… to give… death a place': Rejecting the 'ineffability' of the Holocaust: the work of Gillian Rose and Anne Michaels." *Journal of European Studies* 30:120 (2000): 353-368.

Pember, Mary Annette. "Trauma May Be Woven Into DNA of Native Americans." *Indian Country Today Media Network*, May 28, 2015, http://indiancountrytodaymedianetwork.com/2015/05/28/trauma-may-be-woven-dna-native-americans-160508.

Perry, Bruce D., and Maia Szalavitz. *The Boy Who Was Raised as a Dog: What Traumatized Children can Teach us about Loss, Love and Healing.* New York: Basic Books, 2006.

Porter, Jack Nusan. "Holocaust Aftermath: Continuing Impacts on the Generations." *Journal of Psychology and Judaism* 6:1 (1981).

Punamäki, Raija-Leena, Samir Qouta, Eyad El Sarraj, and Edith Montgomery. "Psychological Distress and Resources Among Siblings and Parents Exposed to Traumatic Events." *International Journal of Behavioural Development* 30:5 (2006): 385–397.

Pundik, Herbert. *In Denmark it Could Not Happen: The Flight of the Jews to Sweden in 1943.* Jerusalem: Gefen Publishing, 1998.

Rashkin, Esther. "The Haunted Child: Social Catastrophe, Phantom Transmissions and the Aftermath of Collective Trauma." *Psychoanalytic Review* 86:3 (1999): 433.

Rashkin, Esther. *Unspeakable Secrets and the Psychoanalysis of Culture.* Albany: State University of New York Press, 2008.

Raskin, Richard. *Life is Like a Glass of Tea: Studies of Classic Jewish Jokes.* Aarhus, Denmark: Aarhus University Press, 1992.

Ravel, Aviva. *Faithful Unto Death: The Story of Arthur Zygielbaum.* Montreal: Worker's Circle, Arthur Zygielbaum Branch, 1980.

Ravitz, Jessica. "Silence lifted: The untold stories of rape during the Holocaust," CNN, June 24, 2011, http://www.cnn.com/2011/WORLD/europe/06/24/holocaust.rape/.

Redlich, Egon and Saul S. Friedman. *The Terezin Diary of Gonda Redlich.* Lexington: University of Kentucky Press, 1992.

Reiter, Andrea. *Children Of The Holocaust.*, Portland, OR: Valentine Mitchell, 2006.

Rochelle, Melotek. *Qualitative Research With The Second Generation: The Effect Of The Holocaust On The Adult Children Of Survivors.* Ann Arbor: UMI/Proquest, 2004.

Rodriguez, Tori "Descendants of Holocaust Survivors Have Altered Stress Hormones," *Scientific American* 26:2, February 12, 2015, https://www.scientificamerican.com/article/descendants-of-holocaust-survivors-have-altered-stress-hormones/.

Romanyshyn, Robert (2010) "The Wounded Researcher: Making a Place for Unconscious Dynamics in the Research Process." *The Humanistic Psychologist* 38:4 (2010): 275–304.

Rothschild, Mary H. "Transforming Our Legacies: Heroic Journeys for Children of Nazi Perpetrators." *Journal of Humanistic Psychology* 40:3 (2000), 43–55.

Samuels, David. "Do Jews Carry Trauma In Our Genes? A Conversation With Rachel Yehuda," *Tablet*, 2014, http://www.tabletmag.com/jewish-arts-and-culture/books/187555/trauma-genes-q-a-rachel-yehuda.

Sartre, Jean Paul. *Anti-Semite and Jew: An Exploration of the Etiology of Hate.* New York: Schocken Books, 1995.

Segev, Tom. *The Seventh Million: The Israelis and the Holocaust.* New York: Holt Paperbacks, 1991.

Semel, Nava. "And the Rat Laughed." In *Sexual Violence Against Jewish Women During the Holocaust,* Hedgepeth and Saidel, eds. Lebanon, NH: University Press of New England, 2010.

Senor, Dan and Saul Singer. *Start-up Nation: The Story of Israel's Economic Miracle*. New York: Twelve/Hachette Book Group, 2009.

Shulevitz, Judith. "The Science of Suffering." *New Republic*, November 16, 2014, https://newrepublic.com/article/120144/trauma-genetic-scientists-say-parents-are-passing-ptsd-kids.

Sigal, John J. "Resilience in Survivors, Their Children and Their Grandchildren." *Echoes of the Holocaust* 4 (1995).

Sigal, John, et al. "Holocaust Aftermath: Continuing Impact on the Generations." *Journal of Psychology and Judaism* 6:1 (1973).

Silverman, Max. "Horror and the Everyday in Post-Holocaust France: *Nuit et Brouillard* and Concentrationary Art." *French Cultural Studies* 17:1 (2006): 5–18.

Snyder, Timothy. *Black Earth: The Holocaust as History and Warning*. New York: Tim Duggan Books, 2015.

Staniforth, Jesse. "'Cultural Genocide'? No, Canada committed regular genocide," *The Toronto Star*, June 10, 2015, https://www.thestar.com/opinion/commentary/2015/06/10/cultural-genocide-no-canada-committed-regular-genocide.html.

Stannard, David E. *American Holocaust: The Conquest of the New World*. New York: Oxford University Press, 1992.

Tal, Kali. *Worlds of Hurt, Reading the Literature of Trauma*. Cambridge: Cambridge University Press, 1996.

Tolle, Eckhart. *A New Earth: Awakening to Your Life's Purpose*. New York: Penguin Books, 2005.

Truth and Reconciliation Commission of Canada. *Honouring the Truth, Reconciling for the Future: Summary of the Final Report of the Truth and Reconciliation Commission of Canada.* The Truth and Reconciliation Commission of Canada: Toronto, Canada, 2015, http://www.trc.ca/websites/trcinstitution/File/2015/Findings/Exec_Summary_2015_05_31_web_o.pdf, 1-6.

Ungar, Michael. "A Constructionist Discourse on Resilience: Multiple Contexts, Multiple Realities Among At-Risk Children and Youth." *Youth and Society* 35:3 (2004): 341–365.

Vaul-Grimwood, Marita. *Holocaust Literature of the Second Generation.* UK: Palgrave MacMillan, 2007.

Wardi, Dina. *Memorial Candles: Children of the Holocaust.* The International Library of Group Psychotherapy and Group Process, Routledge, 1992.

Weisel, Mindy. "Memorial Candles: Beauty as Consolation." *American Studies Journal* 55 (2011).

White, Michael. *Maps of Narrative Practice.* New York: W.W. Norton and Co., 2007.

Wiesel, Elie. *After The Darkness: Reflections On The Holocaust.* New York: Schocken Books, 2002.

Wiesenthal, Simon. *The Sunflower.* New York: Schocken Books, 1998.

Wiseman, H.B., et al. "Parental Communication of Holocaust Experiences and Interpersonal Patterns in Offspring of Holocaust Survivors." *International Journal of Behavioural Development* 26 (2002): 371-381.

Wiseman, Hadas and Jacques P. Barber. *Echoes of the Trauma: Relational Themes and Emotions in Children of Holocaust Survivors.* New York: Cambridge University Press, 2008.

Woititz, Janet Geringer. *Adult Children of Alcoholics.* Deerfield Beach: Health Communications, Inc., 1983.

ACKNOWLEDGEMENTS

My deepest gratitude is extended to Dr. John Rijsman, former Dean of Tilburg University, who gave me the most important gift possible when he encouraged me to write generatively without compromising my emotional honesty. I am indebted to Dr. Mary Gergen and Dr. Kenneth Gergen, leaders of Taos Institute, whose world stance of Social Construction inspires so many around the globe, as it did me. My heartfelt gratitude is extended to Marij Bouwmans, whose creativity and wisdom inspired me and helped me dig deeper, exposing my inner creativity and hidden knowledge.

This subject led me to insightful conversations with fellow explorers: John Dione, Dr. Yossi Tal, Quynh-Tram H. Nguyen, Moira Grayson, Margot Cameron, Danielle Silverman, Linda Watt, Frances Kirson, Laurie Cardinal, Zieva Konvisser, Dr. Herb Merrill, Vanessa Lindores, and so many other kindred spiritis.

I am deeply grateful for the honest, open hearts and creative minds of the original dialogue participants: Abigail Hirsch, Kathi Bailey, Bela Friedman-Kotler, Sylvia Sklar, Judith Maier, Pnina Felder, Leah Meshulam, Dov Spiegler, Dr. Itzik Lichtenfeld and Dr. Yossi Tal. They reinforced that magical transformations really do happen in groups.

A special thank you to my editor, Suzanne Nussey, whose expertise was invaluable and whose deep understanding of what I was wishing to say assured that my wishes would come true. A special thank you also goes to Pamela Schreiner for her meticulous contribution to the accuracy of the research documentation.

A shout out goes to John Fanning of La Muse artists and writers retreat in France, where I set out on my writing journey with *The Inheritors* under my arm.

I would like to express my gratitude to Hebrew University for providing me with an Asper Scholarship that enabled me to conduct research and run dialogues in Israel.

I am continuously grateful to my kind brother and fellow Inheritor, Morris (Morrie) Arian, with whom I shared our family trauma.

I have faith in the resilience of my Third Generation Inheritor children, Alexander and Natalie Baack; Hillary Baack, my daughter-in-law who has embraced our family trauma; and my Fourth Generation Inheritor grandchildren, Finley, Nikolai (Niko) Baack and arriving soon, grandson number three. Go do good children.

A REQUEST FOR HELP
TO FIND MY FAMILY MEMBERS

I am seeking the family of my grandfather, Aaron Koretz, born in Krakow. He traveled to the US, possibly to Minnesota, before the war. My father, Zygmunt /Zalman Arian, and his mother did not join him for fear that the grandmother, Beila Arjan, could not survive the journey. That is why my father was raised under his mother's name.

I am also looking for the family of my great-aunt, Regina Seligman, who lived in California. Their son, Hymie Seligman, married Thelma, a Catholic, and their children are likely still living in California.